County Council

Libraries, books and more . . .

Please return/renew this item by the last due date.
Library items may be renewed by phone on
030 33 33 1234 (24 hours) or via our website
www.cumbria.gov.uk/libraries

Cumbria Libraries
CLIC
Interactive Catalogue

Ask for a CLIC password

Harrison Birtwistle

HARRISON BIRTWISTLE

Wild Tracks

A conversation diary with
FIONA MADDOCKS

FABER & FABER

First published in 2014
by Faber & Faber Ltd
Bloomsbury House
74–77 Great Russell Street
London WC1B 3DA

Typeset by Agnesi Text
Printed in the UK by CPI Group (UK) Ltd, Croydon, CRO 4YY

A CIP record for this book
is available from the British Library

ISBN 978–0–571–30811–8

2 4 6 8 10 9 7 5 3 1

Remembering Sheila

Contents

I have always felt that I have had a music in my head that didn't exist. I wanted to write a music that would retain its mysteries and never become familiar.

Harrison Birtwistle

Illustrations

The author would like to thank the following people and organisations for permission to reproduce their photographs. Every effort has been made to trace or contact all copyright holders but any omissions or errors will be rectified at the earliest opportunity.

Birtwistle as a boy in the North East Lancashire Military Band
courtesy of the Birtwistle family

The North East Lancashire Military Band *c.*1948
© East Lancashire Concert Band

Birtwistle in his National Service days
courtesy of the Birtwistle family

Birtwistle in army uniform
courtesy of the Birtwistle family

The 'Manchester Group' as students
courtesy of Harrison Birtwistle

Portrait of the composer as a young man
courtesy of the Birtwistle family

Birtwistle at Cranborne Chase
© John Vere Brown/Mander and Mitchenson/ University of Bristol/ArenaPAL

Birtwistle's three sons
courtesy of the Birtwistle family

Birtwistle with Elizabeth Wilson and Radu Lupu
© Clive Barda/ArenaPAL

Birtwistle with Michael Tippett in Rotterdam
© Co Broerse

Birtwistle with Melinda Maxwell
© Richard Hubert Smith

Birtwistle with Pierre Boulez
© Betty Freeman

Rehearsing *Bow Down* with Tony Harrison
© Nobby Clark/ArenaPAL

Birtwistle on the set of *The Second Mrs Kong*
© Roger Bamber

Birtwistle at home
© C. Lienhard

Birtwistle preparing *confit d'oie*
© C. Lienhard

Harrison and Sheila Birtwistle
© C. Lienhard

Cowchop 2012
© Adam Birtwistle, with thanks to Piano Nobile Gallery

Drawing on pastel (1995)
© Tom Phillips RA (private collection)

Birtwistle at home in Mere
© Eamonn McCabe

Birtwistle walking on Whitesheet Hill
© Tom Mustill

Introduction

Harrison Birtwistle had a good working title for this book: 'Structured Mutterings'. 'You structure; I mutter,' he said, summing up the conversations we held over a period of six months between mid-March and early October 2013. That was only half the truth: much of the time he structured while I muttered.

Somehow, out of these encounters, mostly at his kitchen table in Wiltshire, we made a path through his life – one route of the many that could have been taken. Inevitably much has been omitted, while certain topics have recurred because they happened to be a current preoccupation. Beethoven is a good example: his name crops up again and again, yet he is not a composer I would have expected to dominate.

I have left these meanderings intact. As far as possible our conversations are presented as they took place. That is to say, rather than ordering the material by topic, I have retained the overlaps, jumps and, on occasion, repetitions or dead ends. I thought this the most faithful way to represent Harry's voice and way of thinking.

Early on he asked me if I would speak to 'other people', suggesting a few names. At first I resisted, arguing that this was his account, not anyone else's. I revised my view after seeing that there was a way to drop observations on particular subjects into the conversation. In some cases, as with family members, they joined in as I interviewed Harry.

Our conversations are also diverted at various points by the pieces on which he was working at the time, notably a new piano concerto for Pierre-Laurent Aimard. I have tried to persuade Harry to describe the process: mentally, physically, musically. The writing of the piano piece is one of many strands running through our talks. However, this book does not aim to give close analysis of compositional structures and techniques, except in so far as the conversation led that way. Those seeking such accounts may find them in several other books, including those by Jonathan Cross and Michael Hall.

The decision to publish the book in time for Harry's eightieth birthday came late. As a result, we packed in as many conversations as possible within the short time available. Hence the decision to plunge in and see where we ended up, rather than plot and get nowhere. I am grateful to Harry for being so ready and willing, and for asking so few questions about the nature of the book or its progress. Quite often he has asked, jokingly, 'Yes, but how big is it?'

I have tried to represent his speech patterns. Certain words have a particular colour. Usually Harry says 'yes'. When he slips into 'yeah', meaning and tone are different: variously ironic, bleak, comic or, occasionally, final. So I have left those in. Similarly, some word repetitions or, occasionally, slight misuses, which would not ordinarily survive in a published piece of prose, are here left intact to convey the ebb and flow of the conversation. I have not worried too much about exact dates – as when Harry has misremembered when a childhood event occurred. For those concerned with chronology, the timeline at the end (based, with thanks, on one prepared by Jonathan Cross for Boosey & Hawkes) will correct or pinpoint.

It seemed important to let Harry relate things according to their personal significance or the connections they now suggest, just as he is happy for his sons to have their own versions of a family anecdote, never mind exactly what happened. If this seems insouciant on my part, it reflects only a wish, where this remarkable composer is concerned, to convey not so much the data as the essence.

On 21 January 2014, Harry rang with some late news. 'I've finished the piano concerto! And decided the full title. It's called *Responses: sweet disorder and the carefully careless*. It's what the piece is about. Very Paul Klee, don't you think?' Very Paul Klee maybe, but very Harrison Birtwistle too.

Fiona Maddocks, 2014

21 March 2013

MERE, WILTSHIRE. HEAVY SKIES, UNINTERRUPTED
RAIN, COLD EAST WIND. TEMPERATURE 5 DEGREES C.

In many almanacs, 21 March is the official start of spring. This bitter, grey day feels like midwinter but the Birtwistle house is warm and comfortable. The stone building was once a silk factory, in a narrow street in the middle of the town. It is approached through a grille-like gate up a single flight of iron stairs, recessed from the street. Thus the ground floor of the house is above street level. The deep slope down towards the entrance acted as a loading bay for carts to access the raised floor level directly, when the house was constructed, circa 1800. Attached on one side to an irregular terrace of small houses from the same period, it nevertheless has a feeling of privacy, solidity and quiet.

Our first conversation, like many subsequent ones, takes place at Harry's kitchen table. The room is L-shaped. All the cooking activity takes place in the upright of the 'L', where windows look down onto a pedestrian lane: schoolchildren pass beneath the window at regular intervals, their cheerful shouts easily audible. Harry likes the sound of young life, the better for needing no attention. Because the room is above street level, only the heads of tall adults can be seen through the slatted blinds as they pass. The kitchen is well ordered, modern and spotless, surfaces clear and gleaming. Someone comes in each day to do housework but Harry clears away first anyway. He feels threatened by mess.

The dining area is in the foot of the 'L', where windows look out on the west-facing garden. A long table made of poplar, commissioned from a carpenter in France when the Birtwistles lived there in the 1980s, stretches nearly the length of the room. This is where we sit. The paint colours are those of stone or sky. Contrasting bands have been painted round the door frames by Harry, with advice from his youngest son Toby (or perhaps it was the other way round). All is simple and sturdy, light and contemporary but not tubular.

One exception to the general plainness is the sofa at the end, which is covered in leopard-print fabric. This piece of furniture once belonged to Robert Graves – 'apparently', Harry says. 'That's what his widow told me. Or at least, he used to sit on it anyway.' (He would explain how this came about in a later conversation.)

The end of the dining area, beyond the sofa, continues round, open plan, to the hallway and stairs, so perhaps the space is actually more of a 'U' than an 'L'. On the street side of the house, mirroring the dining area, is a rectilinear, library-like room. Harry might be found there sitting on the sofa, watching TV or going through piles of admin papers which he tosses on the floor. Not for long, though. A need for order soon gets the better of him. Where does he put the papers? 'In a drawer under the bed. Then I never look at them again.' By mid-afternoon, when most of these conversations take place, this east-facing room always looks dark. Harry says it is filled with light in the morning, and he once had a plan, short-lived, to eat breakfast there each day.

Outside, under the sullen sky, the trees look bare and melancholy. The long straight garden slopes up slightly from the house then drops down to a long, stone water feature, like a section of a canal, except that the water is moving, tumbling down to a yet lower level at one end. This rill is full of mirror carp. The garden design is the work of Lorraine Johnson, who is married to Harry's agent of forty years, Andrew Rosner. Two gravel paths either side of the water lead to steps up to Harry's wooden studio at the end: the impression is of entering a tree house. The whole effect is enclosed, compact, considered, designed. Houses overlook just yards away, but you soon forget them.

Given the weather, on this first occasion we stay in the kitchen. Irvine Hunt, whom Harry has known since he was in his teens when Irvine, four years older, was already a reporter on the *Accrington Observer*, is in the next room. He has come to stay for the week. He often does. 'It's good when he comes. He does everything. I can get on and work.' Drawings and watercolours by Harry's oldest son, Adam Birtwistle, hang on the wall behind the sofa. There are works by other artists elsewhere, including some small, delicate watercolours by Harry's late wife, Sheila.

A French armoire made of elm and 'messed about a bit', as Harry puts it, contains glasses. The dominant piece of furniture is a big wooden chest of drawers painted a dark, dusty blue. Two earthenware bowls from Afghanistan, which arrived unsolicited in a consignment from a carpet-seller, sit formally on the table and contain lemons. There are always lemons on the table and if not lemons, limes, or sometimes both.

What are your earliest childhood memories? Set the scene of your first home, your parents, your upbringing.

Sunday afternoons. That's what comes to mind. They were different. We didn't have much room. I remember a big chassis pram pushed under the table. It was my pram, so this might be one of my earliest memories. I had no brothers or sisters. One end of the pram stuck out. When my son Adam was born we had the same kind . . . And I used to push it under the table, half sticking out, in exactly the same way.

Why were Sundays different?

There was a sort of melancholy. Everything stopped. There was nothing. It was significant even for people who didn't go to church – an idea of 'Sunday best' right down to the clothes and the tea service. I remember the cups we had – they were very 1930s, straight 'triangular', with green lines round the top. My mother went to the Methodist chapel. Or maybe it was Baptist – one or the other. No one knew the difference. I went to Sunday school. I was taught the piano by someone called Ormerod. You can't forget a name like that. Somehow I knew he was homosexual though he was married and though no one had told me about such things and I didn't know the word . . . Those things went on . . . you just knew, though no one said anything. I was never told the facts of life. But I'm not making it up. He once made a pass at my father – when he, my father, was about eighty! My father!

[4]

[By now Harry is laughing helplessly.]

But I didn't go to the chapel until later when I played the hymns. I think my mother was very keen on my having Sunday suits.

Tweed suits, or what?

Tweed suits didn't come until my rebel days. I suppose they were serge or similar, with short trousers for quite a while.

Did both your parents work?

My parents had what was called a confectioner's shop in Accrington [Lancashire] but really it was a bakery. They baked, both of them. I think they had gone to some sort of night school, or done apprenticeships, to learn the skill – how to make bread commercially.

The downstairs had three rooms where most of the other houses in the row – terraced 'two-up two-downs' – had just the two. Upstairs we had a bathroom, with a bath and wash-basin. I remember the roll-top and the big straight taps which were fixed so the water ran very close to the edge of the bath. I can see the green-grey limescale mark. It was probably the only bathroom in the street. But the toilet was outside in the back yard like everyone else's.

Two of the downstairs rooms were workrooms – the shop and the kitchen. The third was the living room. It was always full of things to do with the business. There was a three-piece suite but every two weeks there'd be a delivery of great sacks of flour filling the room . . .

I remember sitting in a high chair – another of my earliest memories, which is very vivid – and being given lumps of dough to play with. Instinctively I still know how bread should be kneaded and pulled. I can watch someone doing it and know if the result will be any good or not. But that tactile thing of working with dough carried through to my abiding interest in clay and pottery. The idea of turning raw material into something else was part of the appeal.

We had a car, too, which set us apart. My father was quite entrepreneurial. I used to go off with him to the farmers beyond Clitheroe – the Trough of Bowland as it's known – and get eggs and butter. There was a place called Lane Ends, just a crossroads . . . Sometimes we'd come back with a load of live ducks or chickens so we could sell our own eggs. I can tell the kind of chicken from looking at an egg. And I can tell which hen in a coop laid it by the markings.

So you were, within that Lancashire mill-town community, better off than some of your neighbours?

Oh yes, certainly. In a small way my father made quite a bit of money because of the war. He dealt in what I suppose you'd call the soft black-market economy, getting hold of and selling things that people wanted. You weren't allowed to have all that dairy produce because of rations. Once we came back with a crate of live ducks and he sold them to someone in Accrington.

As the baker and confectioner in a small town, was your father a well-known figure in the neighbourhood?

I suppose so. A bit. He used to make all the wedding cakes – the sort with three tiers and columns and a bride and groom on top. My mother didn't do that. That was his department.

Were you close to your father?

We were different kinds of people. Or maybe in fact we were very similar but our paths diverged, and the context of our lives made us seem more different than we really were. I was his only son, his only child. That was important in defining how we were with one another. He was a dreamer, full of ideas and fantasies. He was called Fred. His brother was called Harry.

What was school like?

I'll come back to talking about school . . . when I know you better. It's difficult stuff.

We'll come back to it, then. What images or sounds dominated at that period?

Clogs. I used to lie in bed early in the morning and at a certain time, maybe around seven a.m., there'd be a tremendous clattering in the streets, getting louder and louder, and it was the sound of clogs. Workers were on their way to the mill. Half an hour later the same would happen again, maybe for a different shift in another mill.

[One of the chief employers in Accrington at that time was Howard & Bullough, makers of textile manufacturers' machinery used in cotton mills.]

There were people called 'cloggers' who mended, like cobblers. There was a repair shop for clogs. You didn't leave them there. Instead you sat, in your socks, on a long bench with other people waiting while they had your clogs redone. They had metal strips, like horseshoes, that needed replacing. I remember sitting there holding my clogs.

I started at the church school in Accrington when I was approaching my fourth birthday. So, at the age of three, I remember my first proper shoes were a pair of clogs. And they rubbed the skin in deep gouges off my heels, so badly that the teacher had to cut the flapping skin off.

What were your parents like? What sort of background did they come from?

I wish I'd asked my parents more about their past. My father, Fred, was born in 1896. So he was seventeen in 1914 when he went into the war. He was at Gallipoli, and the Somme, and survived both. I don't know anything about his life after [the Armistice] and before I was born, in 1934. It's quite a long time but we never spoke about it. I've got his records from the First World War. He was quite tall as I remember, at least five foot ten or more. But he's down as measuring five foot six and three-quarters. He was just a boy, still growing, when he went to war!

I think he attempted to educate himself, perhaps without much success. He was interested in music. He tried the cello and I think took singing lessons, neither with much success. He went to the Accrington Clef Club [founded in 1903, all-male membership until 1990] which took classical music very seriously.

Tell me about your mother.

My mother – Margaret, always called Madge – was maybe five years younger. I know they lost one or more children, miscarriages I think. Nothing was ever said. But I was a wanted child. She had me, for that time, quite late – I think she was in her thirties. Her background was that her parents were local carpenters and coffin-makers. I never met any of my grandparents, maternal or paternal. They were all dead. I knew some of my mother's brothers. There was a problem to do with the break-up of the family business. I never knew much about it. But I was aware of tensions. Tom and Edgar, two of them, ran the place and lived either end of what we thought of as the 'kingdom'. Edgar brought this chest of drawers – which I painted blue – to the house.

Here in your own kitchen it actually looks quite French?

No. The table is French. The armoire is French. But the drawers were from Accrington, from Uncle Edgar! It was a dresser then, with compartments and shelves above. There were four brothers, and later two stepsisters. I had the impression that my mother kept them all together. I think I was nearly called Edgar.

[9]

So not Edgar, but why were you called Harrison? Isn't there a
mystery about your name?

I don't know if I was registered on my birth certificate as
Harrison or Harry. Harrison was my mother's maiden name.
No one ever calls me Harrison except, when I was a child, to
be posh – or unless they don't know me. But in some reference books my name is down as Harrison Paul, which it isn't,
and never has been. I don't have a second name.

That happened because there was some bother with a
landlady once and I used the name Paul – it was a long time
ago – and Audrey Goehr, Alexander Goehr's first wife,
thought that was my name. When she was secretary of the
ISCM she filled in my *Who's Who* form with Paul on it and
I've never changed it. But it's wrong.

Were you close to your mother?

I don't know. With your parents you accept everything as the
status quo. That's how it is. I mean she would have laid herself
down for me if I'd asked her to. And sacrificed anything. I
think she was sixty-nine when she died, more or less. My father
was older than her. And he was eighty-three when he died.

Was there any music at this stage? What do you remember?

In Accrington there was a military band – the East Lancashire
Military Band, which I played in. That was very unusual.
There were many brass bands but none in the area with
woodwind except ours. I'd love to know what the history of

that was and how that happened. One of the players lived in the next street and taught clarinet. So when I was seven, I started on the C clarinet. It has a sweet mellow sound. It was easier to play because it was smaller. Haydn wrote for the C clarinet . . . Music came into my life.

No starting off on recorder then?

Recorders really didn't exist as instruments for children at that time. All that came later, as part of a desire for school-children to learn music and all those Dolmetsch and Schott plastic recorders.

The introduction of music in my life was very much the ambition of my mother. She was the one. It's not the sort of thing I would have asked for as a child – can I have a clarinet? – no, not at all.

Did you hear music as well as play it?

My father had a radiogram – a radio with built-in gramophone. I remember Richard Tauber singing Schubert. I remember one of Mendelssohn's *Songs without Words*. And the 'Donkey Serenade'. I never forgot the lines: 'There's a song in the air/But the fair señorita/Doesn't seem to care/For the song in the air.'

What else did you hear on the radiogram?

John McCormack, Josef Locke. It wasn't until much later that I had an idea of music as something outside, bigger than the sort of thing I did in music lessons.

Did you take to the clarinet quickly?

I don't think, with hindsight, I was a natural as an instrumentalist or, really, as a musician. I was the only one doing it. It's what I did. Whether or not I had talent didn't really come into it. The thing about practice making perfect is misunderstood. Practice can help the untalented or the mediocre improve. But those who are naturals never practise. That's how it seems anyway. Alan Hacker never practised [the clarinet], nor John Ogdon [the piano].

But I did. I worked hard at the clarinet, and soon after we got a piano too. And I think it was a sort of ambition of my parents that music would be a route I'd take. It was seen as something to aspire to. And coming from that sort of society, they thought it was a form of education too, and that you didn't really need any other sort of studying.

Were you good at the piano?

I played hymns at the Methodist chapel – maybe when I was thirteen or fourteen. I can play [Beethoven] Op. 49 no. 2.

[Deadpan. This is one of the 'easy' Beethoven sonatas recommended for Associated Board Grade 5 students.]

Did you start writing music at this stage?

In retrospect, I can see that as I learned to read music and to understand about notation, so there was a sort of creativity at work – I made efforts to write my own music.

It sounded like nothing. I wrote single lines and I've been doing it ever since!

Did you stay at the bakery? Do you remember the Second World War? What happened next?

My father was a fantasist, a great one for picking things up then dropping them. My mother wanted a bungalow – a newfangled idea at the time. Just after the war – I suppose around 1946 – my father gave up the bakery. It was still a shop until a few years ago. Once I went back, with a film crew making a documentary, and I asked if I could stand in the living room. The fireplace was there. It was like stepping instantly into a lost past, especially finding the cupboard to the side of it which you opened by pressing down a catch – all so completely familiar.

It had a very strong effect on me. It unlocked a memory. This is all very important to me, this sense of time and memory.

Anyway we left the bakery. I don't know why, maybe there was some tension about it, and my father bought a small-holding, a sort of farm, and kept pigs.

Did you move far? Was it a completely different world for you as a young child?

It seemed like the end of the earth but it was only about six or seven miles away.

I thought it was absolutely wonderful. It seemed rural to me though I suppose it was only semi-rural. I remember hearing corncrakes. I didn't hear them again until I went to the Outer Hebrides with my son Silas, just a few years ago. The minute we stepped out of the plane I heard a sound I hadn't encountered since about 1949 or 1950 in Lancashire. Corncrakes. I think they are largely extinct in England. That's the only place where they thrive now. But what I'm really talking about is memory. It has no sense of time. Instantly I was in that place of my childhood.

There's a lingering sadness in me about what happened to that part of the world, where I grew up. The more I was there, the more I became disillusioned. I remember once sitting with some boys . . . and I said, 'Did you know there's been a war?' – imagine asking that! – because it felt so far away from anywhere. It was probably about five miles from Accrington.

Then, when I was there, they built a huge power station, with huge cooling towers.

[The Mayor opened it on 11 May 1956. The station closed in 1984 and the cooling towers were removed in 1988, leaving the shell of the power station, which has since been comprehensively vandalised. If you Google images of Huncoat Power Station you see desolate concrete surrounded by what looks like a quarry lake and rich, green vegetation, once Harry's Arcady.]

Now it looks like a Tarkovsky film set. *Stalker*? *Solaris*? They've taken the towers down but sort of left it to rot.

The house we lived in had probably started out as out-buildings rather than a domestic dwelling. My father spent maybe a year converting it into a bungalow – that bungalow thing again! – but it was the most *Cold Comfort Farm* place you could imagine. The walls were thick and damp. There was no damp course. There was even a shower, but no one used it.

The conversation ends abruptly. We have spoken for an hour and Harry has had enough of reminding himself about a long distant past. We agree to continue the next day.

22 *March* 2013

WILTSHIRE. STORMY RAIN, STRONG EAST WIND.
TEMPERATURE 6 DEGREES.

Harry is listening to a CD when I arrive. 'I didn't think you listened to CDs,' I say, remembering past observations on the subject. 'I don't. Never. Well, I do sometimes. Self-evidently. These Lawes fantasias are wonderful. I listen to Purcell fantazias, Cage sonatas. Maybe early stuff. Machaut. That's it. More or less. I get sent things.'

Today's conversation takes place in Harry's studio at the bottom of the garden. We make the short, blustery walk from the house, up across the raised lawn passing a bed of *Helleborus orientalis*, the Lenten rose also known – appropriately for this raw day – as the winter rose. There are self-seeding *Helleborus niger* too, also called Christ's herb, clove-tongue and Christmas rose. These plants are steeped in myth and folklore: used in witchcraft for summoning demons and responsible for the death of Alexander the Great. No doubt Harry is well aware of this sort of thing.

The studio is functional but rigorously organised, glazed on one side only, tall bamboo brushing against the window and giving a sense of privacy. The other walls are bare slatted timber, a grander version of a garden shed. It is warm and carpeted, practical rather than decorative, long built-in desk, an electronic piano keyboard, table, sofa, huge hardboard panels on which to support the large manuscript paper Harry prefers. Pencils, ruler, sharpener, toolbox, small English dictionary are near at hand.

He has scribbled the names of the twelve disciples on one of the hardboard panels, a reference to his opera *The Last Supper*. Two or three postcards are propped up: one of John Wayne as the Ringo Kid in *Stagecoach*, for reasons which become clear later; another showing the hilly landscape in the Lot region of France where he lived in the 1980s.

Harry pulls out a sheet of printed music headed *The Tempest* – the song 'Full Fathom Five' – and sings it, playing the simple piano accompaniment on the twangy electronic keyboard. 'The only piece of music that remains from my National Theatre days. I could sue them,' he says. All the music from his time as a composer for the National Theatre, where he wrote the music for Peter Shaffer's *Amadeus* and Peter Hall's production of *The Oresteia*, has, Harry thinks, been destroyed.

Apart from the dictionary, the only printed matter is a miniature score of Berg's Violin Concerto, Stravinsky's

Canticum Sacrum and a piece by Ginastera, title obscured by other papers.

Tell me more about your early experience of music, your first music lessons. Were you immediately hungry to explore the repertoire?

Gradually music became, in a sense, my future. It was the thing I was going to do, and if I didn't, what would I do instead? But I think I was doing it without any real facility. I was perfectly good. I became a capable instrumentalist, of considerable technique. I could play anything. Yet it never seemed natural. I worked hard at it. It was all about technique. The clarinet doesn't have much repertoire.

It wasn't until much later that I discovered music as something outside myself.

Was most of your time spent on music? What else did you do? Sport? Anything you'd call a 'hobby'?

I was very much a loner, particularly in the environment in which I lived – the so-called country, at Childers Green. There was a farm near by. I had a friend there, a year younger, who was a natural at everything. He could play the piano better than me. And he never practised.

What I'm really talking about is my relationship with music . . .

What do you mean?

Well, I suppose I'm talking partly about a particular event – a concert I heard with, I think, the Royal Liverpool Philharmonic Orchestra conducted by Walter Susskind. Perhaps it was an ENSA concert. They played [Debussy's *Prélude à*] *L'Après-midi d'un faune.*

That was an epiphany, a real epiphany. The music was independent of me, of my learning the clarinet or the piano. But it's really all about school. I'm not ready to talk about that yet.

OK, we'll leave school aside. Do you want to jump ahead further – to once you got to college in Manchester?

No, it's all about school. That's the essence.

But you won't talk about it now? Well tell me, instead, what your childhood bedroom was like? What did you keep in it?

I can remember it as if it was yesterday – I'm talking about the room in the smallholding. It was when I became a sort of naturalist. To me it was almost an Arcadian paradise, that period as a child – not that I'd have thought in those terms. I used to cycle out, towards the moorlands to the west and the drystone walls and farming area to the east. It was close to the borders of Yorkshire, near Fountains Abbey.

I never liked the idea of hobbies. I seem to think that everything that's ever interested me – moths, which I collected, clay, music – they're all part of one thing. Not something you start to do when you've stopped doing something else.

At one point I enrolled in a night-school class to do clay modelling. But being of a sensitive nature, when the other boys used to flick pellets of clay at me I didn't know what to do, so I stopped. I suppose I was in my early teens.

It was a funny journey, the school thing, because by the time I was about fourteen I had outgrown my teachers. There were no facilities at the school.

So on Mondays I was allowed to go to Manchester to have lessons with musicians from the Hallé. Oddly enough one of them was a clarinettist who came from Accrington. We used to use studios in Forsyth's piano showroom. Later I used to take my girlfriends there. I used to play the piano with one hand when it all got a bit too quiet so no one would wonder what was going on . . .

The conversation ends. Harry retrieves his iPad, a new acquisition with whose function – as with computers and mobile phones in general – he is relatively unfamiliar. But he knows how to search music on YouTube and quickly finds Josef Locke singing 'Galway Bay'; John McCormack, perfect syllables and pure-toned with endless high notes in 'I Hear You Calling Me'. Roy Orbison, one of Harry's favourite singers, is another choice: 'Only the Lonely'.

Then he finds John Travolta dancing with Uma Thurman in the twist contest scene in *Pulp Fiction*, to Chuck Berry singing 'You Never Can Tell'. Harry is hooked. 'You see, he's not moving his head. Look. It's just his hips and legs.' As I shut the door behind me and clatter down the iron steps outside, I can hear the strains of Dusty Springfield belting out 'Son of a Preacher Man'. Given the popular perception of Harry as the hard voice of modernism, this sequence of all-time-favourite balladeer romantics is almost quaint.

4 April 2013

WILTSHIRE. LIGHT SNOW. BITTER NORTH-EAST WIND. TEMPERATURE 3.5 DEGREES. THE 'COLDEST EASTER ON RECORD' HAS JUST PASSED AND THE WORST MARCH SINCE 1962 IS OVER. APRIL SO FAR IS EVEN BLEAKER.

The grass has been cut. The light is spring-like but the ground remains rock hard. Harry's granddaughter Mimi is working at the kitchen table, preparing for GCSE exams. One of her exam subjects is music. Harry has cast an eye over the checklist of information she is supposed to absorb and can hardly believe it. Later over tea he bellows, 'Define serialism. Define serialism! What the hell does that mean?'

Today he is already in the studio, slumped and cocooned in an animal-print blanket against the cold, as if in a sleeping bag or chrysalis. This could be a metaphor for the fragmented conversation that follows. There are many long silences, for all that it might look fluent on the page.

Some days I find it easy to talk about things . . . Others I clamp down. I can't tell why or when. The other day I stepped in at short notice to cover for Max [Peter Maxwell Davies] in a workshop with young composers in Wales. It felt as though I was – not in any big-headed sense – in control, doing something I never imagined I would be able to do: standing up and talking to a lot of people.

I have a great sense of the 'imago'. You know what an imago is? Creatures who are born fully formed. The butterfly is the obvious example. There's no middle period, no development except of course at the chrysalis stage. They arrive in life, perfect. There are people like that. It's not a good thing or a bad thing. It's a fact.

I was not like that. I never felt that anything came naturally. I was always struggling, in ways that perhaps no one really saw, to get to where I wanted to be – though I didn't absolutely know where that place was. These things are hard to express . . .

[Long silence.]

Since our last conversation, you have started your piano concerto. The songs you were finishing for Mark Padmore [Songs from the Same Earth] *have already been published. I can see the new score, propped up on the piano. The guitar piece is complete, too. This is a lot of work in a short space of time. Yet you say you struggle.*

The guitar piece was short, more an 'occasional' piece. The songs had been a longer process, since last year. So long, in fact, that I set one of the poems twice as I'd forgotten I'd already done it. I took it in to Boosey's and they said, 'You've already done this.' They've published both.

Did you think about the piano concerto at the same time you were working on these other two pieces, like a big river flowing beneath whatever's happening on the surface?

Yes. Exactly.

You know what's interesting? It's how you introduce ideas. How do you bring in the piano? At the start? Halfway through? Loudly? Almost inaudibly? These are obvious questions but they preoccupy me all the time. You think of Beethoven's Fourth Piano Concerto – the piano is there at the start. Then you're committed. That shapes what comes next. I'm stating the obvious.

Or Schumann's Piano Concerto? You said you had heard that recently and been impressed by it?

Yes. It's a good piece, that. But that's also another matter for me. I am surprised how well I know it, every note. I must have played it – the clarinet part, I mean – in an orchestra once.

I suppose in the intervening years – since first hearing it – I've accumulated and been dealing with things, as a composer. So I now recognise or perhaps appreciate better what's in this music.

You see that picture?

[Three small images of John Wayne in *Stagecoach* (1939), a cowboy classic directed by John Ford, on a page torn from a book, are stuck on Harry's work board. The film, shot in Monument Valley on the Arizona–Utah border, is an archetypal Western, with a rousing if repetitive soundtrack based on cowboy songs.]

The question is, how does the director introduce John Wayne? How? He isn't there at the beginning. It starts with all these disparate people inside the stagecoach. The stage is leaving. They're wondering where Ringo is. No one knows. Then suddenly the driver says, 'Hey, look, it's Ringo.' He's where you least expect him – standing in the middle of the highway, off his horse.

The 'dolly' that pulls the camera can't keep up with him and there's a point when John Wayne's face is out of focus. And then he's in focus again. They're the stills in the picture I've got pinned up. It's a fantastic way of setting it all up.

Those moments, where you set something up, are sacred – then you're committed. It's like the first mark on a canvas. Everything you do next is a result of that. You can control the size of a canvas and the scale of the piece but that first mark is your only free choice. Every move after that is a consequence. I think a lot in terms of moves.

Moves as in chess?

Yes. Francis Bacon talked about how he didn't want to make pictures that were about anything. He said that within two minutes you were going to be bored of the subject. I agree.

The process of introducing things – where we started talking a moment ago – and making a context is all part of the game.

You know how Britten introduced Billy Budd in his opera?

Remind me.

He has him name himself: 'William Budd'. That was a brilliant solution.

Music isn't like painting. It's linear. So you might have a big notion of where you are going but you can only achieve it note by note, bar by bar. You can't make a big splash of colour like you might with paint. Not that that's how all painters work, but there isn't even that option available in music.

So how do you keep that sense of – what can we call it –

Momentum? Engaged state?

That kind of thing. How can we keep that alive all the time as you introduce events and make moves?

I'm talking subjectively. As always.

So how do you create something which is in a permanent state of exposition? This is what matters. This is what keeps me awake – metaphorically. This is what the battle is.

To what extent do you plan? You have been thinking about the piano concerto for a good while.

I could never design a piece externally. Never make a 'form scheme' like Stockhausen. There are certain things, ideas, which are thrown up which you would never arrive at if you followed a preordained plan.

So it's risky?

It's like making up a recipe. You go to the store cupboard.

You decide to get out certain ingredients. You might start with raisins, and then get out the mustard.

Not nice –

But you're already sunk. That's what you have to do and you have to be very clever to avoid disaster. Those are your ingredients and you have to make them work together.

That's what I think about all the time. All the time. Day and night.

You have to work with surprises. You can't fabricate them. The sum total – the raisins and the mustard and what you do with them – becomes the form. Not the other way round.

Think of Beethoven. Nowadays I have a completely different feeling about Beethoven in a way I couldn't have felt in the past. He's a composer who never, ever does what you expect him to do. And what he does is never contrived.

There's an early piano sonata I heard someone play the other day – No. 11 [Op. 22 in B flat major] – it's a bit like an embryonic *Hammerklavier*. I thought it was extraordinary. In one sense you know the harmonic language but everything seemed new, as if for the first time.

In some ways these thoughts have made me qualify my feelings about music I don't like. Or didn't like. Or didn't think I liked. But not about the ones that don't speak to me in some way.

What composers go into that 'don't speak to me' category?

Tchaikovsky.

You don't get it, or what?

I don't get it? Oh yes, I get it all right. That's the trouble. I'm not interested in it.

And others you do – or don't – get?

Rachmaninov. He doesn't do what I'm interested in.

Not even those great, lavish clarinet solos – as in the slow movement of the Second Symphony?

It's all too subjective.

Then does Mahler go in that category too?

With Mahler there's an element that has to be admired. When I first heard the First Symphony, I was particularly struck, especially by the first movement. It wasn't like anything I'd heard. It seemed to be music from left field as they say in America. (Do I mean 'left field'? Is that what they say?)

Where did you first hear Mahler 1?

In Manchester. The Hallé played it under John Barbirolli when I was a student. He introduced all the big composers around that time – Mahler, Sibelius, Vaughan Williams. I remember being taken with VW's Sixth Symphony.

Do you still respond to that repertoire?

When I listen to Vaughan Williams I find it very harmoni-cally undernourished. But there's another aspect to all this: those pieces that made an impact at a particular stage because it was part of a process of discovery, as a young person finding things you had never come across before, that change the way you live, the way you think. They make your life extra-ordinary, because they are so different from everything you've known up to that point. They shape and qualify and offer possibilities you'd never realised might exist.

Are you thinking of particular pieces which made that impact?

It was a big step for me from Vaughan Williams to first hearing Debussy's *L'Après-midi d'un faune*. And later, to Messiaen and to Boulez's *Le Marteau sans maître*.

I was about twenty when I heard *Turangalîla*. I went to London and heard it with Sandy Goehr. It meant a lot to me then. Maybe now it's more difficult for me.

I have to keep coming back to the way all this feeds this thing, this unformed, indescribable inner self which I am trying to talk about. It's a way of finding a way through the labyrinth, the thicket . . . They help you to open gates . . . make you see you are not so stupid . . .

Can we go back to the imago idea, your preoccupation with it?

Part of my problem, or maybe 'problem', has always been trying to hang on to a sense of self while being surrounded by those who seemed more brilliant, and certain of what they were doing. I was never that.

People in my 'circle' at Manchester – Max, Sandy, John Ogdon, Alan Hacker – they were all in a sense so brilliant. The world is full of them.

My difference – something I've struggled with all my life – is that I had an 'idea', and I don't know what you'd call it . . . it all sounds so boastful.

Do you mean a sort of vision, a calling?

Yeah, well.

[Long silence.]

From early childhood . . .
    It all sounds pretentious.

[More silence.]

Did something happen? An experience – good or bad?

Yes. No.

[More silence. Big intake of breath.]

OK.
    I want you to draw a big box round this.
    Get it? A big black line.

[Later I am concerned as to whether Harry wanted me to include this. I felt that he did, compared with other no-go topics which arose where I conspicuously, almost theatrically, stopped the recording and closed my notebook. Yet had I asked him directly, I suspect that in his modesty and privacy he would have said no. So, Harry, I have taken the decision to keep it in. I hope it is the right one. If not, forgive me.]

There's a day I remember. I was about thirteen. We lived near an area of beautiful woodland. We talked about this last time, you remember? It's still there, but it's a bit messed up now, which makes me sad. I used to go that way to school.

That day, I walked along the road, past a lake and into a wood. It was the most beautiful day. Everything looked magical – not in a silly way but just the magic of a perfect day. I didn't go to school that day. I went in the wrong direction.

And I kept thinking how beautiful everything looked.

For what it's worth, and it sounds so arrogant, but on that day I thought, 'I'm going to do it.' Whatever 'it' was. If it hadn't been music it might have been something else.

I wasn't being pretentious. I was too young for that. I simply felt, one way or another, that I had some sort of task, some impossible goal, and that's what I was going to do. The decision was made.

But presumably it wasn't that simple? Do you remember anything else about that day? You didn't go to school . . . ?

No. I don't remember anything else.

No, it comes straight back to the fundamental, the rock-bottom notion of how I am, who I am, and how I am in respect of the imago . . . It's been my fight, my problem. I fought my way from the start because nothing was easy.

And yet overriding all my struggle was the clear sense that I knew what I was fighting for. Do you get me? Maybe it happens to all young people, that moment of self-discovery. The epiphany, the road to Damascus, all that stuff. I didn't discover Jesus that day. But the awareness of that day has reverberated all my life, right up till today, sitting here now – and that's the truth, God strike me down, as they say.

It – what I'm calling 'it' – manifests itself in a lot of other things in me, and the way I live my life. All the things I'm interested in feed into the 'it'. I can't bear the idea of having hobbies – of something you start doing when you stop doing something else. For me, making a pizza or writing a bar of music or boiling an egg or growing a potato or whatever it is, it's all part of the same thing. It has to be the best. I set myself ideals and I am frustrated when I don't achieve them.

Maybe I could have done other things if I hadn't done music – written poems, painted pictures. I don't know. I've picked up certain things – like making pots – and then got rid of them again. I can't be an amateur. Whatever it is, it needs my full attention.

I knew someone who made pots who taught art when I was teaching music at Cranborne Chase [School]. I remember in particular one thing he said: that when you see a pot, you have to decide how heavy it is. And if it surprises you when you pick it up, it's not a good pot. Its external aspect must be the same as the internal. That resonated with me.

These practical considerations are important. It's why I've always been interested in Beaker pottery – it's no different from what you might make today. And in the pots I have bought myself, there is no decoration. It's very difficult, and rare, to see a pot where decoration works. The Japanese are good at it.

So you don't, following that logic, like Greek pots?

I can't bear them. You look at the decoration and then you don't look at the pot. Or the other way round.

Of course an appreciation of all this has taken a long time. I'm being very purist. I like the pure, unadorned statement. It's a kind of Zen thing.

It's always been that way for me. When you are young and in a state of innocence, you can appreciate this aesthetic without necessarily putting it into words.

[Silence.]

Shall we go back to talking about the piano concerto, about starting a piece?

I don't think anyone else writes music the way I do – by which I don't mean what it sounds like –

Though that, too . . .

I mean the way I do it, in practical terms. You see this . . .

[We look at three large sheets of manuscript paper, neatly notated in full orchestration. The opening bars have fast-note castanet machine, crasher and triangle. The harp plays two Es and two F flat harmonics – 'so four notes the same, four strings all playing the same note' – then the piano enters. Harry picks out the piano part on the electronic keyboard he uses, seemingly set to honky-tonk mode. Other sheets of manuscript, less fully worked, are attached to other hard-board panels on the other side of the workbench.]

The piano comes in very near the start. You made that decision. Here it is, after just three bars . . .

Yes, it's like an interruption. It's marked *'brillante'*. I don't know what those percussion instruments will sound like together.

A sort of shimmer effect?

Something volatile. I can sort of guess what it sounds like but I won't know exactly till I hear it.

But what I mean about not doing what anyone else does – and I'm not talking about better or worse – is that I have all these little bits, and I might put them in any order, and then I have to copy out what I have stuck together.

Copy out?

I mean I have to do it in neat, correctly, so that I know where I am and what I'm doing. And that becomes the piece. Otherwise it's a mess, or a confusion, and it doesn't feel real.

Like a writer typing up something they've written in longhand?

Maybe. It helps pin something down. There are so many possibilities, and in the end you make a pact with the idea and you see it through. And when you hear the piece you're not going to hear my problems, my struggles. It's going to sound natural, as if it's meant to happen that way, each note following the other as naturally as an apple falling off a tree.

I don't believe in inspiration. When people say, 'Oh, that was my moment of inspiration', it usually means they've lifted the idea from someone else.

If they found a toad and then painted a picture of a sunrise – now, that would be inspiration.

[That conversation, for now, is closed. After a pause, we move to easier topics.]

Can you see a starting point, in these pre-Manchester years, for an awakening of interest in the specifically 'English' traditions in your music – which surface particularly in your music-theatre pieces from Punch and Judy *to* Under the Greenwood Tree *to* Yan Tan Tethera *to* Gawain?

Yes and no. Those interests were always there. I never really searched for them. I don't think I had any more contact with Punch and Judy than any child who goes to the seaside in their summer holidays.

But most summers as it happens I did spend in Fleetwood, near Morecambe, with my mother's stepsister. My mother would take me and then I'd stay there for maybe a week or more – I can't remember. They – my aunt and uncle – ran an ice-cream shop. They made the ice-cream with real ice in a big churn.

Did you like the ice-cream?

I can't remember anything about it.

Once again, when I was there, I was on my own. I didn't know anybody. There was a puppet show on the beach, and it took place in a sort of big box, as big as this room. It was run by a man and a woman. I can't really remember much, but they didn't always do the same story – it would say on a board outside what that day's tale was.

Most days I'd just go off on my own for the day. I did get friendly with a girl who was a bit older. We lost touch in the way of those passing childhood friendships. Next time I encountered her, when we were about sixteen, I found out she'd become Miss Morecambe! All amazing long legs and high heels. She was called Dorothy Peak.

Miss Morecambe! Did you think 'wow'?

I thought wow.

But those other English, pagan, folk traditions – I don't know. Some things just strike you. In a way, the things I have dealt with in theatre have not required a decision. The choices have almost been automatic. I haven't had to agonise. There's a sort of continuity in them, in the subjects I've chosen, but I don't know how that continuity works.

As a child I used to make stage sets – little ones, without any reference to a particular dramatic scenario or play in mind. They were completely abstract. One was all black and pink.

My chamber opera *Io Passion* [2004] directly relates to that way of thinking. I mean it started almost as an installation. I just had an idea of an area in two halves – the inside and outside of a room.

[He draws a rough outline of two boxes marked 'out' and 'in' with a couple of arrows.]

We – Alison Chitty the designer, Stephen Plaice the writer, and I – mocked it up in the rehearsal room and worked out some action and I said, this is about a man and a woman. The woman is inside and the man is outside. I just heard they're doing it [*Io Passion*] in Australia . . .

What set me going is that you see someone putting a letter in the door from the outside at the exact moment it comes through the door on the inside. That's the kind of thing that fascinates me.

You know classical music has become debased. This is another subject, for another day. There's a battle somewhere, a desire for classical music to be simple, in two-minute sound bites. And people say, 'Why doesn't he/she write music like John Williams?' [*Starts la-la-ing the theme tune to* Star Wars.] You see. It's all two-minute soundbites. You know they play concerts, whole concerts, of this stuff . . . ?

We've talked a bit about beginnings. What about endings?

Endings can be a big problem. How do you get out of something? One reason I'm often disillusioned with pulp fiction – thrillers – is because people don't know how to end things. You get landed with a subject matter and you have to find an exit. Quite often with thrillers I get near the end and then I stop reading because I can see how it's going to finish.

But that's why the film *Pulp Fiction* [Quentin Tarantino, 1994] is so good. It manipulates the narrative by beginning with the end but of course you only know that in retrospect. The end is in two halves, A and B. A is at the beginning, B at the end. You begin to understand how it works once you've got used to it and can analyse it. I've watched it many, many times.

Film was always part of your life, even as a child? Did you go to Saturday-morning flicks or the equivalent in Accrington?

Yes, there were several cinemas in Accrington and I went, often on my own, but the event I really remember was a special Sunday thing – one of the rare, melancholy Sundays when something actually happened. Two doors along there was a family with five children – seven people in a two-up two-down. God knows how they fitted in. I distinctly remember we all went off to a special Sunday-afternoon cinema club at the Hippodrome, which wasn't usually a cinema but a place of live entertainment, music-hall.

[The live entertainment included a nude revue until 1955. Built in 1908, it was demolished *circa* 1960.]

I remember it was freezing cold. No heating. The film was *Alexander Nevsky*. I like to think it was the first film I ever saw. When, many years later – possibly even sixty years – I watched it again, I remembered every single thing about it: the soldiers picking up children by one leg and putting them in the fire. The Teutonic Knights – Nevsky draws them onto the ice then the ice cracks . . .

So the score was by Prokofiev? Quite a major film score to begin with. Did you notice it particularly, or recall it?

Not especially. It wasn't what made the impact but I did study Eisenstein's *The Film Sense* quite carefully and, as it observes, at one point the music imitates the contours of the lances. The film affected me hugely. I was very young. It must have been just around the end of the war so I was about ten. There was an element of loss of innocence too. Afterwards, they showed a film about Belsen. I remember sitting there and thinking the Second World War was to do with winning the war and the glory of it. Instead they showed a concentration camp . . . That had a devastating effect. Ask Tom [Phillips]. He remembers the same.

[Tom Phillips recalls being taken by his mother to see Walt Disney's *Bambi* in Clapham, only to be horrified by the newsreel images – described by one news headline as 'Scenes Worthy of Dante'. Ian Buruma's recent book *Year Zero: A History of 1945* (Penguin, 2013) makes a similar point, describing how British moviegoers unable to stomach the atrocities before their eyes on the screen tried to walk out of cinemas, only to be turned back by British soldiers at the door telling them to go back and face it. Neither Tom nor Harry, however, remembers troops.]

What, then, was your own impression of war? The Second World War began six weeks after your fifth birthday and ended two and half months before your eleventh. Was Accrington bombed?

A bit. Not really. The way I experienced it, war was fun. It was all a bit of an adventure. They were bombing Manchester twenty-two miles away but we didn't hear it. We were given gas masks at school.

Were there Anderson shelters?

I suppose there must have been some. I do remember air-raid shelters going up at the start of the war. You couldn't fit an Anderson shelter into our communal back yard! But at my infants' school there was a family who must have been fairly well off because they had their own shelter built. They were tailors called Carr. They had a daughter called Marie. I think I had a bit of a crush on her. It was my first sense of girls being different.

Your Siegfried moment? 'Das ist kein Mann'?

My Siegfried moment.

[I mention, as we finish the conversation, that I am going the next day to Glasgow to see Scottish Opera's *Der fliegende Holländer*.]

There's some wonderful music in it. I like early Wagner – *Tannhäuser*. And *Lohengrin*. But *Dutchman* – why don't they cut that silly spinning song?

11 April 2013

WILTSHIRE. SKIES ARE BRIGHTER. FOR THE FIRST TIME SINCE THESE CONVERSATIONS BEGAN, THE WIND HAS MOVED TO THE WEST. TEMPERATURE 12 DEGREES.

Miniature red tulips are flowering at the base of a young gingko tree, still in a pot. Harry has been pruning a row of quince trees on raised ground above the fishpond. He notes that they have to be trained in a wineglass/fan shape. 'Then that's it. I'm never going to prune those again in my life. Done.' Three mallards are taking an undue interest in the pond. He aims an experienced guttural roar at them and they scatter. 'They made a nest on the wall. The ducklings hatched. Some fell one way, some fell the other. They die very quickly. The stupid duck sits in the middle and doesn't know which way to go!'

Jochen Voigt, a regular visitor, is in residence. His life partner was the late Peter Heyworth, my one-time predecessor as music critic of the *Observer* and a close friend of Harry's. It was through Heyworth that Harry nearly came to write an opera with W. H. Auden. Harry recalls: 'I went to meet Auden at Peter's flat in Bryanston Square. He was very keen on *Punch and Judy* and thought the libretto [by Stephen Pruslin] was the best since *The Rake's Progress*! I remember him saying that a good libretto should have the simplicity of a dumb show that is activated by the music and the text. He asked me if I wanted to write an opera on *Love's Labour's Lost*. I said no. I wanted to write one on the ancient myth of Er, who was destined to eat his own children. Auden wasn't too interested.'

Harry is feeling off-colour today, without any particular symptoms. He has a book about Raasay in Scotland written by someone who was his neighbour there, which has made him melancholy. He nevertheless proceeds to talk fluently for fifty minutes. The conversation takes place in the studio. The newly published score of *In Broken Images* is on the desk.

You see this.

[He points to a quotation from a Robert Graves poem of the same name – 'In Broken Images' – at the start of the score.]

He is quick, thinking in clear images;
I am slow, thinking in broken images.

He becomes dull, trusting to his clear images;
I become sharp, mistrusting my broken images.

These lines – the entire Robert Graves poem – seems to say it all . . . a battle against fluency.

You didn't hear this piece did you? I mean in the Queen Elizabeth Hall when it was premiered. Tom Service interviewed me. You were at the dinner . . .

[The world premiere, at the Queen Elizabeth Hall on 24 May 2012, coincided with a dinner for my husband Tom Phillips's seventy-fifth birthday. Harry was due to join the dinner after the concert. Tom's portrait of Harry is in the National Portrait Gallery. A big drawing, also by Tom, in fiery orange colours and made of short wild markings, hangs halfway up Harry's stairs. The night of *In Broken Images*, Harry's wife, Sheila, was in hospital, nearing the end of a long illness.]

Sheila died that night at about exactly the time this piece finished being performed. I swear to it on God's truth! Exactly the same time. The call came just after.

Strange. These things happen that way . . .

This piece is like a dry run for the piano concerto, how one bit relates to another. You see it's laid out in blocks so you can see exactly what's going on. It's a bit like a graphic score.

Like a George Herbert poem. Or e.e. cummings.

Yes.

You said you have, or make, small elements, and that you might then put them in a random order. Like a collage? Like Schwitters?

I like there to be a sort of inner logic. It's not a question of being deaf or blind to where the pieces go. I don't simply take a pair of scissors – which I have done in my life. I don't do that any more. I think a lot about how one element relates to another. If you were painting a picture, the question is always what colour would this be . . .

I have to be able to define these very strong, contrasting groups that you can see here on the page.

[He points, again, to random sections in the score, hurriedly turning pages in search of particular examples.]

So the blocks aren't necessarily instrumental?

No, though they are contrasted obviously by the basic colours of woodwind, brass, strings, percussion. And it's quite severe. I have to be severe with the material. But there are inner contrasts, which are not just the groups I've just described but, as it were, the music within. So there's brass which is very loud here, very quiet there . . .

The tempo is different. Each element has an identity. When they start combining, the identity – of that brass bit we just looked at, for instance – is retained. It never loses its identity or changes, right through the piece. It remains discrete. It never disintegrates or merges.

So if you look at this music, and I really do mean *look* at it, you see there's an attack there [*pointing to a brass chord*]. And there's no attack there [*he points to a chord straight after*]. And there are attacks here, here, here [*he stabs his finger, attackingly, through a few bars*] and none of them are playing together. So what they're doing is hocketing.

[42]

A medieval technique [in which phrases are broken by rests, so that when one part is silent, another fills the gap] *you've used many times before . . .*

I have, yes. The whole piece is a hocket. So a journey between them makes a line, but individually – say that this here [*pointing*] is an increment of two, this is an increment of three – they are linked yet they also have an independence. The whole piece is like this.

[He turns more pages, so it's hard to keep up. I note down, randomly, 'p. 18'. Harry hardly draws breath. Even though it is hard to know precisely what he means, without having the score there to follow, his train of thought has its own coherence and I have left it intact. Those bars may no longer exist, yet this is perhaps the closest we come to seeing him in full creative mode.]

For instance this section here, within this woodwind bit, they play high/low, yes? And the parts in the middle are common to both. So there's a line going like that [*up*] and another going here [*down*] and this here [*indicating another part*] doesn't belong to anything. Nothing synchronises . . . So it's like a sort of, I don't know what you'd call it.

There's a dependence, yes? And an independence too, yes? So if you played that bit, it has a logic, a continuity.

I think it's rather good, this bit. It's quite energetic. There's a lot going on, a lot of energy. Here, I introduce for the first time another element – something which is lyrical, smooth ['p. 18']. So to say again, there's a continuity. I knew

I was going to introduce this 'colour' but I didn't know when. So we're looking at music that is about a third of the way through the piece. And then the woodwind is 'legato'. It's a melodic technique. Things are beginning to happen . . . [*Chuckles.*] But I'm very severe with the ideas. It might not be noticeable to anyone else. But it's noticeable to me, yeah?

But these processes or procedures, as you describe them, are in keeping with what you have always done in your compositions?

Yes. But I'm freer. Freer in what I'm doing than I was. I used to use tables and charts . . .

But previous to this I think I was very self-consciously looking back for a while. This piece doesn't belong to that. I wrote a violin concerto, a piano trio. And I wrote an oboe quartet, and a thing for cello and piano . . . I mean looking back not to my own work but to musical history, just dabbling with it. It was just a moment. I couldn't do it again.

I don't think anyone else is doing it like this. Are they? I mean, tell me, are they?

I couldn't possibly answer about the exact technique. But it certainly sounds different!

Does it? That's good. That's all I care about. [*A dark chuckle.*]

I know you've been spelling it out in the way you've talked about In Broken Images. *But please spell it out again, for clarity.*

It's this question of having, in order to retain and deal with these elements – and this is a pretty radical, I think, way of dealing with it – I have to be quite severe with myself. That word, severe, again. So that in a sense it's making conditions that . . . oh dear, I'm not doing very well, am I?

Go on. You were saying you are making conditions –

I have to be strict with the ideas in order to hang on to the essential, basic issue of what the piece is about. These blocks of material play a game. They keep their identity. They fuse in some ways. In other ways they don't.

But if you look at the piece again, here, two-thirds of the way through, you can see that there is an independence, and it's fusing. Not growing, exactly.

Amassing?

I have no words.

The above outburst continued, almost unprompted, for nearly an hour, and has left Harry exhausted. He needs to go back to thinking about his score. I leave him to it.

19 April 2013

WILTSHIRE. SUNNY, LATE AFTERNOON. STRONG
SOUTHERLY WIND. TEMPERATURE 12 DEGREES
BUT FEELS COLDER.

Harry has just woken from a post-work snooze. He has a woolly-mammoth look, heavy-eyed, arms akimbo, cardigan on top of many layers of clothing, protection against the cold wind.

We sit at the kitchen table. He flicks through a book of photographs about the art of masquerade in Zambia, Haiti, Burkina Faso and elsewhere: *Maske*, by Phyllis Galembo and Chika Okeke-Agulu.

Many of the figures are in full-body disguise, swathed in wood, material, dyes, transforming them into strange spirits of the forest. At all the ones that look most buried, or forest-like, or like a walking tree, submerged beneath branches and leaves, Harry says: 'That's me. That one's me.' After some ritual making of tea – pale green, served in plain white porcelain beakers ('I hate tea bags, loathe them') – he wakes up properly and gets straight to the point.

We've talked about how to introduce ideas. I was thinking about that in relation to my opera *The Last Supper*. How do you introduce Judas? The disciples are singing the Lord's Prayer. They leave a gap at the end. Judas walks in, unnoticed, and sings the Amen. That was straightforward.

But how do you introduce Christ? We contrived a

situation where everyone speaks in riddles. I can't remember exactly how we did it. They ask questions. They move into a huddle and from the middle of that huddle, Christ steps forward and answers the question.

What was the riddle?

I can't remember. It doesn't matter. I think the answer was 'the wind'.

He's there in the mêlée. You haven't seen him enter. He is revealed.

I think there are riddles in all my operas. In *Punch and Judy* it's 'Riddle me ree' . . .

And what is the answer?

It's a cherry. But I don't think that's in the text. There are riddles in *Gawain* too . . . actually I can't remember that one either.

You are thinking of Gawain's trials?

Maybe.

[That subject closed, he takes a smart, fancily wrapped chocolate egg left over from Easter, smashes it within its bag and divides the spoils, only slightly disconcerted to find the chocolate is white. The remainder of that day's conversation, on tape, includes the sound of crunching.]

So I was allowed to leave school on Mondays to go to Manchester, to something called the Northern School of Music. I've said that, haven't I?

Can we, yet, fill in the years between the three-year-old in clogs and the fifteen-year-old going off for clarinet lessons in Manchester?

I knew you'd ask me that, you bugger.

OK, let's go on with Manchester.

So I was younger than the rest. They were eighteen-year-olds. There was a special class for doing the scholarship exam. You could sit for a county major scholarship to music college where you got all your fees paid, and your subsistence and your grant. I wasn't eligible to take it – I can't remember why. I think you had to have GCEs and things.

I applied on my own and was the only person who got one. I couldn't have it until I was eighteen. I had an amazing two years when I'd left school. Well, I'd sort of left it already. Well . . . I didn't go much actually.

You mean you played truant?

Sort of.

[Silence.]

During those two years I became totally enlightened. I discovered everything in the way you can only do at that age.

[48]

By myself. I read a lot of literature. Things suddenly clicked. I remember devouring Aldous Huxley, Sheridan Le Fanu, lots of verse, especially A. E. Housman and the other war poets, and Sidney Keyes.

Did anyone guide you? Where did you discover what to read?

Bookshops, libraries. Maybe I had a bit of money too.

In the daytime I was working to earn a living, building council houses in Accrington.

In the evenings I was playing in bands, amateur music-making really, in the Accrington Hippodrome. But the nice thing was that while it was amateur dramatics we were professional players. We did all those terrible pieces – *Lilac Time*, *Kiss Me Kate*, the one with the Mounties – you know, [*croons*] 'When I'm calling you-oo-oo-oo, oo-oo-oooooh . . . with a love that's true-oo-oo-oo-oo-oooooh . . .' *Rose Marie*, that's it.

And of course, Gilbert and Sullivan. I hated G & S. All of it. Sexless theatre. Awful stuff. But I was paid. It was an eleven-piece orchestra – piano, string quartet, bass, clarinet, flute, trumpet, trombone, percussion. Everyone took it very seriously.

Each show was a week's run. That was fine. Then came the pantomime season. I was hired to play but only on condition that I played saxophone. I had £65 saved up to buy a motorbike, a BSA Bantam. Instead I bought this bloody saxophone. I bought it one week and played it the next.

As the pantomime season progressed, into January when the audiences started dwindling, they started cutting the band, till there were fewer and fewer of us in it.

I remember it ended up with a percussionist, a trumpeter, the pianist and me. And we went on to play in the variety shows – when you had a conjuror and a comedian and girls who stood around in feathers. In the end the trumpeter was dropped too, so it was just the three of us.

The great star locally was a character called Frank Randle. He was quite famous, the same generation as George Formby and Gracie Fields. He was banned from the BBC because his material was too risqué and a bit subversive. He made films too, and had a thing in the *Beano* called 'Randle's Scandals'.

[He was celebrated for throwing his false teeth into the audience, and once bombarded Accrington with toilet rolls. He toured his show, *Randle's Scandals*, round the country but by the mid-1950s was facing bankruptcy, and died in 1957.]

Norman Evans was another of those northern entertainers. He had one-sided conversations and a show called *Over the Garden Wall*. It was all mother-in-law jokes and dressing up as women and medical complaints – very northern, and a prototype for Les Dawson.

So we played in what was now a trio – me and the pianist and percussion – in between. They'd have their material. But there was a whole procedure of filling in which you just knew. In order to get continuity they'd shout out 'Happy for tabs', and that's to join up one thing for another. There were things like 'pom tiddly pom-pom, pom-pom'. We'd just play that. I liked that best.

*You were still living at home, but must have felt liberated, work-
ing with older musicians? Suddenly a man, not a child?*

I didn't know what a man was! I went on playing in these
bands through college. It was seasonal work.

You mean playing in Manchester?

No, in Accrington. I didn't have a career anywhere else.
[*Chuckles.*] It was really fourth-rate rubbish. But somehow I
feel it was an amazing route into theatre. It got me going
about the idea of theatre. I wouldn't like to say precisely how.
    Of course everyone else I played with in these shows was
much older. I was definitely the young one. I was always the
young one. Stravinsky said something like, 'All my life I've
always been the young one. And now I'm the old one.' Yeah.
There's nothing in between.
    So to finish on the scholarship – you could get back
papers. I played in the Lancashire County Youth Orchestra
and I was one of the few who was likely to become a musician. There was someone, I think he was the county music
organiser, took a shine to me. Or, rather, took an interest in
guiding me. I remember him well, and I think I owe him a
lot. He said I should apply. I think it was quite a tricky thing
to do. I mean the questions weren't the sort you got on the
school curriculum, and you were supposed to have 'A' levels
or whatever they were. Questions like, who is Hindemith . . .
The only access then to Hindemith – to use him as the
example – was on the Third Programme, if you happened to
catch it.

I put some compositions in with my paper. You sat the exam in Preston. No one knew. Not even my parents. They had supported me to that point, of course, but I suppose it would have been hard for them financially if they'd had to pay.

If you got through the written exam, you then went to play. I played some Finzi and Stravinsky's Three Pieces for Solo Clarinet.

Therein lies a tale. That first Stravinsky piece, which was called 'Pastoral' originally, I think, was a 'moment' for me. I don't think the other two pieces were so interesting. But that first one has cropped up a hell of a lot in many guises in the music I've written, certain aspects of it. I know it had a collection of pitches I'd never heard before, or played. It's short, just one sheet of paper. It's a bit like the opening of *The Rite of Spring* [composed five years before the Three Pieces, in 1913]. You know the opening of *The Rite of Spring* isn't 'by' Stravinsky? It's a folk song. I've heard choirs sing it. It's the context in which he puts it, and the register, that makes it extraordinary.

But I've often thought the acciaccaturas or whatever they're called – the crushed notes – in Stravinsky are non-decorative in the way they relate to the harmony. In tonal music they belong to the harmony. Or there are harmonic resonances, or dissonances which are resolved. So in Stravinsky they are non-functional. I think Boulez, for instance, uses them a hell of a lot, these non-functional decorations to the note. They are like satellite notes. But I like to think that I identified that myself very early on, no thanks to Pierre Boulez. Great minds think alike . . .! It's been a lingering feature of what I do. In Boulez it becomes the thing in itself. There are sometimes more decorative notes than the important notes themselves.

Can you point to a particular piece of yours in which this happens?

Yes. No. It happens all over the place. It proliferates. If there's anything called style or whatever, it proliferates. It's part of the handwriting, the calligraphy of my music.

From your earliest compositions?

Yes. No question. But that's where I got it from: from that piece of music. Specifically that first Stravinsky clarinet piece. The other two are of no interest. There's another – *Petite Pièce* by Debussy, which is one of the most exquisite pieces for clarinet and piano. I always thought that the piano and the clarinet was a horrible combination. Debussy wrote this piece that made me really think about things. He made a piece which is beautiful, like one of the piano *Préludes*, a very delicate piano part. And also the relationship between the material of the piano and the solo instrument.

But voice and piano don't work too well either, and as for violin and piano – terrible. Awful combination. Naaaaaaaah, na-na-na-na-na-na-na-na – naaaaaaaaah . . .

[He sings the opening bars of Beethoven's 'Spring' Sonata as if with a nasal tin whistle.]

Chalk and cheese. There are two wonderful pieces – the sonatas by Brahms, written for clarinet but also played on viola. I think they work better on viola. I heard Pinchas Zukerman play them on the telly and it was the first time I really thought what wonderful pieces they are. He plays in a style which isn't for the audience. Just as if playing in a room. Wonderful.

The Schumann *Fantasiestücke* and the Berg *Vier Stücke* – those and the Stravinsky and the Debussy were the pieces I loved to play. And there were ideas in them that somehow carried forward into the next stage of my life. I'm sure no one else was playing the Berg at that time. I never heard anyone in England doing them. People like Jack Brymer – one of my [clarinet] teachers – would never have done.

How did you know about the Berg pieces?

I was very good at finding stuff.

Were you actively composing at that stage, around sixteen years old?

Yes.

What?

Oh, all kinds of stuff. I don't know . . .

Has it survived?

Maybe. Adam [HB's oldest son] had some, I think. Maybe it's in the British Library. Don't know. Don't want to know.

Is it recognisably your music?

I don't know. Not sure. Don't want to think about it. I really don't want to think about it.

But you don't mind its existence?

Rather it wasn't.

[Silence. The remaining fragments of Easter egg suddenly acquire new interest and become objects of audible munching and silent concentration.]

So the two years before you went to Manchester were like an extended gap year, a period of discovery?

I suppose so, though you don't always realise that at the time. I don't know – I was suddenly aware. It's a very special thing –

To self-educate?

It's not quite that straightforward. No. I suppose some people were influencing me. I'd catch up. I'd hear about something new and say, 'What's that?' If you were to talk to Sandy Goehr and Max they were, I think, rather amused by this nature child.

When I first met Sandy it was as if he had a fully developed intellect. You knew he had a position in the world as a composer but he hadn't yet really written much music – some songs, and piano pieces, and some clarinet pieces for me to play. Because there was still the possibility, or as it seemed probability, I'd be a clarinettist.

Once you met Sandy and Max what happened?

We were like a kind of communist sect. We were all in accord. But my position was that I was the secret composer. The idea of my writing music – I didn't really do it officially until, I don't know, not when I was at Manchester.

I was becoming more and more positive about what I wanted to do, but the possibility of doing it, the practicalities, seemed so . . .

For Max and Sandy there was nothing else they could have done. I could have been an instrumentalist.

Not pianists?

No. Sandy couldn't play the piano much better than me, but Max is quite a fluent pianist. Sandy was at the Royal Manchester College, but Max and Gary [Elgar] Howarth were at the University – as music students.

For practical things, you had lessons at the Royal Manchester College. Gary was a trumpeter and came up through the brass-band world . . . We had access to huge amounts of new material through the Henry Watson Music Library. It was an amazing resource. I used to go there and browse. It's where I must have first come across Boulez's flute *Sonatine* [1946]. I didn't recognise the composer's name and it didn't stick in my mind, but the music did.

Serialism was the tract at that time, a doctrine – which I never felt easy with. Officially Hindemith and Schoenberg were mentioned in the same breath. That was modern music. They were the emblems. Stravinsky was different.

I seem to remember Max switched directions, and maybe even burned some of his early, tonal works.

Did you burn any?

Too secret.

Or too sacred?

Secret and sacred.

In my head there was this dichotomy between the question of writing music and the question of earning a living. I didn't fulfil my potential as a clarinettist. When I was in my first year, I was given all the professional dates as a clarinettist – playing in the Mozart or Brahms Clarinet Quintets and music clubs and things like that. By the end of being there it was like a dying light, when if that's what I was going to do I should have been rising fast, not doing the opposite.

And the idea of writing music was that I could actually do it, and support myself in some way or other – because the only way I could support myself was as an instrumentalist. But I got – I don't know what you'd say. I used to go down to Buxton Spa orchestra at weekends for money, but at the end I was superseded by other players who were appearing, the new breed.

Was it a kind of self-destruct?

Completely. I lost the whole idea of being able to do it, or wanting to do it, or even having the talent to do it. Then it comes back to this issue of practice not making perfect. There were those players who never practised. But I was hanging on by my fingernails because I wasn't like that. I couldn't get away with it.

But you passed your exams?

Oh yes. I played the Brahms Sonata for my matriculation – the E flat. Lovely piece. Too big for the instrument. That's why the viola works better – Pinchas Zukerman *held* it. I don't think I got honours or anything. But I did it. I passed.

Was there much rocking round the clock going on?

Not till I was in the Army. In Oswestry. Royal Artillery. I was twenty-one. Bill Haley came along right in the second year of being in the Army. The mid-1950s. There was a lot of jazz in the Army. I'm very familiar with it. We lived in things called spiders. They have a central ablution thing – toilets and things. Why they call them spiders I don't know, they only have six legs. Maybe there'd be twenty people in each one. One was brass band, another was jazz and the other was posh – classical. I spent my time with the jazz lot. They played jazz records all the time.

Did you like it – the jazz?

Erm. Sort of. OK.

So my scholarship was for four years. I did three in Manchester. And then I went to the Royal Academy to do clarinet. But I'd really given up by then.

So you were a hopeless case.

I was a hopeless case.

And you weren't practising?

I wasn't practising. But I was playing in the first orchestra.

So there was plenty of residual facility?

Yes. But that's when I met Alan Hacker. And I heard him play and knew there was no hope for me.

Did you want that to be the case?

Well, there was the problem of what the fucking hell am I going to do, yeah?

I sat down one Christmas. And I wrote a piece called *Refrains and Choruses*. And it went quite well from then on.

Was that when you were at the Academy?

Yes. And it was played at Cheltenham [Festival, 1959].

Did you submit it to Cheltenham?

Yes.

So some part of you believed in what you were doing?

Yes. I was doing some copying then, for Richard Rodney Bennett. He was a year younger than me. I met him at the Royal Academy with Cornelius Cardew.

I did a concert at the Aldeburgh Festival. I was playing. I played a whole recital. Well, I was pretty good at pitching it: a piece by Malcolm Williamson, and one by Richard Bennett, and one by Cornelius Cardew and Sandy's pieces. I think.

Was Britten there?

Don't know. Can't remember.

But I could play. I hope I haven't given the impression I couldn't. But my heart wasn't in it. One thing was there wasn't much clarinet repertoire. I've told you most of it.

I think it's an interesting journey I made. I had lessons from Frederick Thurston, Jack Brymer and Reginald Kell.

Did these teachers inspire you?

No. I gather a girl I used to travel on the bus with always saw me as a bit of a rebel. She thought I was a Dylan Thomas type. Not alcoholic though.

I was a fancy dresser, you know? You could see me coming. [*Loud laughs.*] That's what my mother used to say: if you go out in that they'll see you coming. I used to sport window-cleaners' jackets piped in red.

What colour were the window-cleaners' jackets?

Well you know. Like window-cleaners'.

I don't know –

Come on. Like pre-denim. Blue. British denim. And my mother piped them in red.

She did them for you?

She'd have done anything for me. They were rather nice. And corduroy suits. Red. Green. You could get them made for practically nothing. You'd get these swatches. And Harris tweed.

And then there was sort of 'Zoot suit' – as in Zoot Sims, bebop or modern jazz players. Long jackets with velvet collars and lapels.

Was it pre-Mods?

Yes. But no one dressed up. I didn't belong to a set. I was my own set, or sect. It's quite a big journey between Zoot Sims suits and Harris tweed suits. They were very different. There used to be a place called 'Fifty-Shilling Tailors' in Accrington. Or Burtons. 'Let Burtons dress you.' You could get suits made for nothing.

I wasn't aware of anyone else dressing like that. I was clean-shaven. My hair was red, a dark auburny red. I was called ginger at school. 'Hey, Ginger . . .'

So you must have stood out on the Manchester bus?

Dylan Thomas! [*Laughs.*]

27 *April 2013*

WILTSHIRE. THE CRUELLEST MONTH REMAINS CRUEL: TEMPERATURE 7 DEGREES, HAIL, SLEET AND SHOWERS, NORTH-EAST WIND. NO LILACS, OR ANYTHING TO SPEAK OF, IN THIS SLOWEST OF SPRINGS.

This short Saturday-morning conversation, at the kitchen table, is characterised by the sound of Harry knocking, cracking, rustling, unwrapping and eating (not entirely alone) another left-over Easter egg. Once again, crunching dominates the recording. By the time we finish, only crumbs remain.

I was talking to Tom [Phillips] about the question of intuition. And talking about jazz players and the fact that they never do anything apart from what you know they're going to do.

Even when they improvise?

Especially when they improvise! That's exactly when you know what it's going to sound like.

You'll have the jazz world up in arms . . .

I know. But I think I know what I'm talking about. Boulez talked about it as well – the same thing – that improvisation is a sort of state of – oh God . . . I, I – what's the word?

Do you know one thing that I haven't probably expressed to you, and that you're probably aware of: I'm *hopelessly* dyslexic. [He says 'dyslectic'.] Essentially, that's a fundamental problem but also a fundamental ingredient of what I am. One thing is true, there have been some pretty great men that have been dyslexic; it has a long tradition. But the question of dyslexia has been invented much later, and only in retrospect has it become an explanation, an understanding of myself. And, in spite of it, it's a major part of what I do, how I am.

But going back to the question of jazz and intuition, or improvisation, and what I remember discussing with Boulez, is that someone once described it as a form of speeded-up composition. But it's not. It's what comes out of the top of your head. Composition is a way in which you can go deeper, through consideration. This is what I mean about the way you can stretch your intuition, through analysis and thought. All the processes I've stumbled across or fumbled across have been a means of dealing with this.

So the simple rhythmical studies at the beginning of Messiaen's *Quartet for the End of Time* – he wrote a lot of other stuff about his theory of composition – but the essential thing is there. It's an examination of a proliferation of ideas. Whereas in improvisation you are stuck with one idea. You can only touch the surface of composition.

In *Carmen arcadiae* [*mechanicae perpetuum*] –

A piece to which you constantly return . . .

Yes . . . So in that piece, I carried a process forward which was hard – it's the opposite of, say, Bach doing *The Art of Fugue* or the *Musical Offering* where he explores things for the sake of technique, though the good thing about Bach is it always comes out as being inventive too. In a way, *Carmen arcadiae* is the essence of that way of thinking. It explores a radical idea, taking something to its ultimate extreme and it's not repetitive. I couldn't use that process for the rest of my life, but ideas in it come into and out of focus.

The truth about anything is whether it comes out of the context of the time, or if it is *of* its time, or if it looks forward from that point in time. I think Jackson Pollock is an interesting example. He was well imitated. Everyone said, that's interesting, I can drip paint too. Let's all drip paint. And so for a while everybody dripped paint. But in a sense the truth of it is that it comes through historical necessity, and context. You can always drip paint, at any time. But it's because it happened when it did.

It's the way most things happen artistically. So you can only create minimalism as a reaction to something which is its opposite.

Do you mean minimalism as we think of it now – Glass, Reich and so on – or do you mean the minimalism of Webern?

I think I mean minimalism now. It's a black-and-white situation. There is an idea of minimalism in music. Or in painting – white paintings or black paintings.

Here's an aside: why is it I am attracted to minimalism in painting but not in music? You've got to know, in minimalism, what it is you're throwing away, throwing in the dustbin, to achieve the minimalist state – a sort of purification. But to me, in music, it's like – what's the milk without cream called? Skimmed milk. It's as if the cream has been thrown away. So much has been lost: harmony for example. You've virtually given dynamic away.

But it's based on chord patterns?

One chord pattern.

So what does it lack?

Tempo. It can only express itself in a rather active tempo. Instrumentation. It's quite baroque . . . Hugh Wood has a book of essays. There's a wonderful essay about Brahms. And there's actually one on my *Triumph of Time*.

I think minimalism's problem is it's too near me. I think it's baby and bathwater. I wanna keep the baby. Or the cream.

[Chuckles.]

This is important. I'm throwing ideas around here. Off the top of my head. It's called wild track, what? You know, as in cinema. They keep the camera on something . . . they might use it or not.

I can tell you something specific about Paul Klee, and the indebtedness in this piece *Carmen arcadiae mechanicae perpetuum*. When I express how that piece comes about, it's non-linear.

In *Carmen arcadiae* I invented, like wild track, say five different musics which had no relation to each other. I didn't consider what the relationship of these various elements was, only that there was a unity because of the harmony I chose. They all belonged to the same harmonic family – like different people within it, each with their own character.

So I made no comparison between them. These ideas were simply written, out of context, with certain unifying features. You can't, say, have a piece which is highly chromatic next to something in C major. That would be silly. So there was an inner unity, which was necessary for them all to belong to the context.

I then, and this is where Klee comes into it, I independently characterised – and this is where it contradicts itself – rhythm, register and dynamics. I can draw it for you. Each section here represents the different elements – 1, 3, 5, 4, 2, say. They don't go one after the other. That's one pattern. Then a new pattern begins, maybe starting with a 5, say . . . And each section will have different lengths They're not all the same. There's a rhythmical differentiation. Do you understand?

[I understand as he explains but cannot be sure whether it will translate into print in a way which the reader will find comprehensible. But for anyone studying the score, it may prove useful, so it remains as he spoke it.]

Then I have an independent line, which is the dynamics: let's say *ff*, *pp*, *f*, and a generalised *mf*. So the rhythm doesn't correspond with the dynamics, and that in turn doesn't correspond to this other independent line which is the register: high and low, which has its own scheme. So all these elements have a sort of rhythm and life of their own.

So everything is moving differently, independently, within the whole, each component never merging? Hence the 'mechanicae'. . .

Yes: so there's the dynamic: high, middle and low, and rhythm. You get it? So I generated a long piece and then I put a line through it. This line was like a circle. I cut out from it.

This makes sense when you hear the piece. We should listen to it. But you know it?

Enough to grasp the point you are making. And after you put a line through this 'circle', you disposed of the rest? How?

Yes, the rest went. And that piece – *Carmen arcadiae* – is the part I cut out, the part that survived. So it was like wild track, the original whole. Maybe it's a pity I threw all that other music away. But no, I was right to throw it away.

I made a circle of manuscript paper round my walls and looked at all the pieces. I was in Scotland at the time.

So this is how it relates to Klee.

How?

Oh, methodology. He re-examined his whole process as if his former world had never existed. He invented his own world. That way of thinking was a direct, if you want to use the word, inspiration. You should ask Olly [Oliver Knussen] about that piece. He's conducted it a lot – and in fact he's conducted a lot of my music over a long period of time . . .

Getting hold of Oliver Knussen, composer, conductor and fount of inspiration for a generation of other composers, is no simple task. As imperatives go, 'Ask Olly' has the feel of the same sort of challenge offered by the *Where's Wally?* children's books. But Knussen is a man of honour, and having promised, he sent these observations by email, tweaked and improved by him three times, a few days after the book's deadline had passed.

When did you first come across Harrison Birtwistle?

OK I read a magazine article about *Punch and Judy*, the idea of which intrigued me very much, and went out and bought the vocal score the very next day and the record of *Tragoedia* shortly thereafter, and I was hooked. I went to Edinburgh to see *Punch and Judy* (I'd been away at the time of the Aldeburgh premiere), and a few months later went to see it again at Sadler's Wells. The original production was beautiful to look at – it was like one of those amazing clocks with moving figures, like the famous one in Prague – and the singers really looked like huge Punch and Judy puppets. I've still got some photos of it that I cut out of that magazine article in that same vocal score, by the way.

The music fascinated me, as did Stephen Pruslin's amazingly original libretto. The component parts of it – the juxtaposition of nursery rhymes, maypole dances and post-Webern constructivist elements (actually more like post-late-Stravinsky now I come to think of it), the sometimes brutally violent and sometimes tenderly beautiful short numbers and chorales, they all felt some- how congruent. To me it wasn't gratuitously bizarre and 'shocking' but something really new and fresh. It was as 'modern' as could be, and would not be what it is without the experience of the Continental avant-garde, but nothing quite this direct and characterful was com- ing out of mainland Europe that I knew of, and that still holds true today – perhaps [Ligeti's] *Le Grand Macabre*, but that was much later than *Punch and Judy.*

Something about it also seemed curiously familiar, to come from an imaginative world I knew something of – whether that's an intrinsically English thing, or whether the toy-shop aspect of Birtwistle's music struck a receptive chord in me personally I can't really say. So I became a major fan – I went to hear every new work I could, as they came out: *Verses* [*for Ensembles*], *Merid- ian*, *Nenia* [*: The Death of Orpheus*], *The Triumph of Time* and so on and on.

When did you first encounter Harry in person?

OK I'm sure he doesn't remember this, but I was introduced to Harry by Colin Davis at a rehearsal for *Nomos* at the Festival Hall in the autumn of 1968, I think. As we are both shy it was a long time before I really felt able to really talk to him – about twenty-three years actually, when he came to Aldeburgh as composer-in-residence in 1991 (a notion that would have been science fiction until a few years before!), and he came to concerts where I conducted *Melencolia I* and *Meridian*. In more recent years he has visited Snape a good deal, and it has been a real delight to get to know him a bit better.

He has unexpected stories to tell about his early musical experiences, like his visit to Vaughan Williams as a boy, going to Barbirolli's concerts (it's a nice thought that when he used to see the Hallé Orchestra both my dad and grandfather would have been playing), and has some equally unexpected perceptions about music he's known for a long time – an example I remember is 'Beethoven discovered the real nature of the bassoon in the Fourth Symphony', or that 'with the *Introduction and Allegro* Ravel actually invented an ensemble', something I've also heard him say about Boulez and *Le Marteau*. Inventing ensembles is something he's done too – think of the bass clarinet and cor anglais trios in *Meridian*. His sensitivity to instrumental characters, colours and weights is exceptionally acute.

Between meetings we stay in touch from time to time – I occasionally send him picture postcards (he rather likes my small handwriting), and he phones up out of the blue now and again. My respect for his strength of character (although he's a gentle person) increases the more I get to know him, and musically too as I've become more aware of the details when I learn his scores, particularly when I eventually got to conduct *Punch and Judy* myself twenty-odd years after seeing it for the first time. Composers will always, I think, be strangely attracted to things which they know they could never do themselves.

How does Harry's music work?

OK Now there's a question! Harry's compositional strategies are so unique and completely personal to him that detailed analysis without recourse to his sketches would be futile. From the outside you can identify elements in play and a sort of general picture of how they are being treated to produce the effect he's after at a given moment in a big work, and for the performer that's probably enough, because the whole apparatus is directed towards the communication of an overall dramatic or formal vision.

Smaller pieces that explore only one or two tactics in depth will have a higher degree of abstraction, however. These are too developed to be called sketches, but the concepts tend to find their way into layers of the bigger pieces. *The World is Discovered*, like several early things, deals with ways of handling rhythmic unisons (irregular doublings of a single line which no one instrument ever

[ok] plays completely), sometimes curiously oblique ones that aren't immediately evident when you hear it. This idea shows up writ larger in the orchestral pieces *Chorales* and *Nomos*, but these are not the whole story.

Carmen arcadiae, to take another example, explores limited rhythm and pitch fields in sharply defined registers – but the resulting machine has such a Heath Robinson-like charm that what is actually a rather severe construction has won a *Sorcerer's Apprentice*-like popularity within the new-music world. And, similarly, it's not difficult to hear variants of the same sort of idea operating as one among many volcanic strata in a huge work like *Earth Dances*.

The point, it seems to me, is that however abstract or mechanical or (ir)rational the processes by which Harry arrives at his actual notes, in his hands they become a language capable of animating a huge range of characters and vivid, powerful atmospheres. That is surely why he is such an exceptional dramatic composer. Perhaps it's also why at the moment I'm particularly attracted to shorter pieces in which this power is evident but distilled, like *Night's Black Bird*, or the new *Moth Requiem* – even a tiny piece like *Dinah and Nick's Love Song*, written on a single sheet of paper, casts a spell in the concert hall out of all proportion to its dimensions. You can find Birtwistle's music 'difficult' or not, or like one piece more than another, but it seems to me that you can't be indifferent to it. And that's the mark of a great artist, I think.

*

[72]

Can we pick up, again, Harry, on how music came into your life at the start — either in early childhood or as you were growing up?

Going back to early on in my life, a book that examines this subject and which was quite important to me was *On Growth and Form* by D'Arcy Thompson [1860–1948, Scottish mathematician and biologist]. I first got to know it early on, when I was about eighteen.

Did it stem from your childhood interest in nature?

Yes. Absolutely. Just as an aside, looking at that book, it qualified a lot of things we've been talking about. Like leaf forms. I just understood them, these forms, in terms of simplified nature study. I didn't understand how they were relevant — or how they meant anything to me. It was just an accumulation of information. And then here is this book, which is precisely about their meaning, which has really gone into the subject and made a scientific thesis out of it.

I was just an amateur and took it as far as I needed it, not quite sure how it would ever be of significance to me. But when you find things for yourself as opposed to being taught, it's how things have a reality. One is taught a lot of things and you don't relate much to them. But when it's your own finding, it comes out of your own preoccupations.

The process of so much education today is that you're just given information, facts. You have to learn it and you have no idea what it's all about or how to digest it.

I'm very insecure about the whole question of teaching — me teaching — and yet nevertheless I've done quite a lot of it and maybe even done it quite well. But I have never done any teaching which is in any way academic. I would never give a lecture on something. Didn't want to, didn't know how to, had no interest. But in a sense, to be put in that position – of teaching – you can mean a lot to some people, and a little bit to most.

But this question of how things become real because they belong to you – this applies to many things and it informs the way I write music. Consequently there are certain stages of the journey of 'my creative life' – God, I wish there was another phrase – where these things come to the top of one's imagination, or mind. They're exactly what you're looking for. Everything becomes clear.

I'm not saying it's unique. It probably happens to everyone.

But this one piece of music feels like one of those moments in which all the ingredients come together. I didn't think that when I wrote it, but I do when I hear it: *Carmen arcadiae mechanicae perpetuum,* an invented, fanciful title. I wanted something which would sound like a Roman dedication, which embraced the contradictions of the piece within it and the piece itself.

You've spoken about that particular piece already. But clearly it represents an important turning point for you, as a composer. Try to explain more, or to explain again . . .

It's contrast within contrast. Context within context.

I wrote it as a direct influence from the work of Paul Klee. Now I'm not in any sense trying to do a musical imitation of twittering machines or anything like that.

It comes down to what we were talking about yesterday. It's about making a chord. I think a chord is a good emblem. How do you make something from your intuition? Oh God, here I go again. I've often thought about trying to formulate this but I don't want to. I'm quite happy it's vague.

[This crucial thought is interrupted first by a phone call and then the arrival of the Polish housekeeper and a long discussion about whether an extra half-hour is owed for last week or whether it should be carried over till next week. We then move from the kitchen to the studio and try to pick up the thread.]

This way of thinking about this piece – I arrived at that radical stance by its context. It opened up a lot of things about the way I went forward as a composer. It seems to me like a sort of focus, a turning point in my career. I couldn't have done that if I hadn't written the pieces I did before. I couldn't have just burst forth out of the blue and thought that's a nice idea, and written *Carmen* like that. I'm making a comparison with the dripping paint.

In exactly the same way Jackson Pollock had to learn to draw first? Or Turner, making the same journey from skilled draughtsmanship to near abstraction?

Maybe yes, maybe it applies to all artists. In a rather idealised way, it's where the truth is, as opposed to people who say 'I was inspired by this or that' and in fact what they do is just take an idea and copy it.

When you say context, do you mean wider historical context too, as well as just the point in your own career? So Schoenberg, atonality, could only come out of nineteenth-century Romanticism?

Yes exactly. Everything. And so-called minimalism couldn't have existed without highly chromatic music first. It's a direct reaction. It's a pity they couldn't have found something more interesting . . .

[Pause.]

You know something. If I write on here three *ff*s on a trumpet, what do you do about three *ff*s on a flute? It's not the same. That's a crucial point.

[Pause.]

You seem to have ended that set of thoughts. How about something practical – these big sheets of manuscript paper you use? Your pencils?

I had tons of these big sheets made. I couldn't believe I would get through it as quickly as I do. Sometimes they're covered in a blizzard of notes, sometimes hardly at all.

The pencils I use are 3B – quite soft and easy to rub out. These click-lead kind I use – like architects have – suddenly die on you and you have to throw them away. I go through a lot of them. The leads are always splintering if you're not careful. They last about a day. Sometimes I can't click fast enough to write down what I want.

Sometimes, too, the little rubbers at the end get wedged in the metal holder – I feel like a surgeon, extracting them like root-canal treatment. Press too hard, they go too far in, then I have to extricate them with one of my various tools – I have a brooch with a pin. Isn't it interesting that you're reduced to that in the middle of something really rather serious.

Then I use this sort of three-sided sheath on the pencil to avoid repetitive strain. They're a bit of a nuisance. You have to boil them to make them white hot and malleable or else they won't slide onto the pencil.

You boil them?

Oh yes. About every six months.

I see . . . do you think everyone who uses these pencil sheaths has a boiling-up session?

[No answer.]

But you know there are also bigger click-pencils, with bigger rubbers? I'm not joking. [*Laughing.*] And you know what the worst thing is? That sometimes they bounce out. But the angle they bounce out at means they can end up absolutely anywhere. You can be working on something quite tricky and important, then suddenly *bdoing!* – it's gone and you have no idea and you're down on your hands and knees when you should be thinking about a complex pulse pattern or harmonic change. Today the rubber disappeared altogether.

Eventually I found it under the piano and finally managed to fish it out by lying almost flat on the floor. [*Laughing.*]

But life's like that. I have a strong sense of the ridiculous.

If you throw a handful of frozen peas on the floor, a lot of them will accumulate close to each other. Some will be a certain distance away. One or two will be ten times further away at the end of the room. I find that really interesting. It's something irrational within something rational. That fascinates me. It's intrinsic to what I do.

The same happened when we watched the progress of bubbles inside a fizzy water bottle, where one went on rolling long after all the others?

Exactly. When I throw food to my fish it ends up in the middle, all in the same place, and mostly it goes away from the centre, like a flower blooming on the surface of the water. That's beautiful.

3 May 2013

CHILLY. WEST WIND, SHOWERS.
TEMPERATURE 17 DEGREES.

A handwritten note pinned to the door says, 'Back 4 p.m. Enter'. It is not yet 3.45 p.m. but there are sounds within. The note, evidently, is redundant. 'More sugar! It needs more sugar,' bellows Harry from the kitchen. His godson, the natural-history filmmaker Tom Mustill, has come to stay. He is attempting to be the sous-chef. Under Harry's tutelage he has made a dressing for roasted beetroot, with oil, balsamic vinegar and sugar. There's a tense but cheerful atmosphere as the cooking takes place. At the same time, together they are concocting nettle and wild garlic soup, the key ingredients gathered that afternoon from Whitesheet Hill, from where they had just returned. Whitesheet, a chalky upland area with ancient earthworks, is a favourite place of Harry's, comprising a Neolithic causeway camp, Bronze Age barrows and a large Iron Age hillfort. It is to the north of Mere.

Tom shows us a picture, just snapped on his phone, of Harry on the hillside, up to his waist in nettles, stuffing a plastic bag with leaves. He praises Harry's attentiveness as a godfather and remembers Harry giving him, on his fifth birthday, a grown-up toaster. In the garden, the quince trees, pruned a few weeks ago, are in leaf. Our conversation, in the studio, is short. Harry has a bad back and despite having managed the nettle-collecting admits he can't really move without pain. Thinking to find a self-contained, straightforward topic, I suggest his work in the theatre.

Shall we discuss theatre today, and your time at the National?

Do what you want.

OK. Did your interest in drama start when you were playing in the pit orchestra in Accrington?

I don't know. I think it definitely did start with all those pantomimes and shows in Accrington.

Had you seen much classical theatre, or read Shakespeare and the rest?

Not really. Nor opera either.

Had you seen any, apart from operetta in Accrington?

Yeah. I went to Covent Garden quite a few times. I remember very well Klemperer conducting *Fidelio*. And I remember Tippett's *King Priam*. I was very keen on Beckett, which I heard on the radio – the Third Programme in those days. Beckett was in the air.

Early Pinter?

No. Didn't like those much.

When LWT [London Weekend Television, part of the ITV network between 1968 and 2002] started, they commissioned me to write an opera, on anything I wanted – that was the start of *Mask of Orpheus* but in the event that didn't happen for a long time . . . It all came through Peter Hall. Humphrey Burton took me to see a poet who'd translated Virgil's *Georgics*. Cecil Day-Lewis? I think it was him. It must have been because I remember asking – rather stupidly – [his daughter] Tamasin Day-Lewis if she was a relation.

I'd got into the subject of Orpheus via the *Georgics* and

did a version at Cranborne Chase – all those girls, and the boys of Bryanston [School] too.

Anyway Peter Hall saw *Punch and Judy* at Sadler's Wells and asked whether I wanted to work at the National. That was the first time I met him. He must have been about to start there.

But around that time – I can't tell you the chronology – before he went to the National, Peter was working at Covent Garden. He got involved with *Orpheus* and under his influence the opera was taken away from television. They were very cross. Peter wanted it to be a film. I was piggy in the middle and probably a bit gullible. Glyndebourne was also going to do it. When I came to finish it a good decade later it was like archaeology trying to find out what I'd been thinking . . .

Anyway, to go back to the National, the *Hamlet* I did with Albert Finney was still in the Old Vic. In the new theatre I did *Tamburlaine*, *As You Like It*, *Julius Caesar*, Ibsen's *Brand* – that was the best theatre music I've written. It wasn't really appreciated but I thought it was good. Then *The Tempest*, *Winter's Tale*, *Cymbeline* . . .

And Amadeus, *Peter Shaffer's 1979 play with Simon Callow as Mozart . . .*

What you couldn't do was take a gramophone record and play Mozart in the middle of the play. So I took various elements and 'treated' it – just the bare bones, using thirteen wind instruments [as used in Mozart's *Gran Partita* K361]. And I did all sorts of funny things with it, though I can't remember what – I used a lot of stuff without the melodies but I didn't write any 'Mozart' as such. I dissected it.

The most difficult bit was when he was supposed to be writing something very famous – can't remember what, one of the iconic works – and I had to have him getting it wrong, then struggling until he got it right, like a Eureka moment. I don't think it would ever have been like that with Mozart. But it was in the text. The received idea of what people do when the right music . . . da-da-da? No, that's wrong. How about da-*dee*-da? Done it!

People haven't a clue about what writing music is actually like.

You were very engaged with every production, weren't you? It must have been rewarding.

It was. But I wish I had done it earlier in my life. It was time-consuming – a proper job. I remember Peter Hall saying you don't have to do all this – getting so involved – but I found it hard not to.

It was all quite a difficult time – I'd moved to Raasay [Scotland] in 1975. I had my own music to write. I probably played a lot of truant but I was inspired by Peter Hall.

Through him I wrote my only film score – for *The Offence* [1972] directed by Sidney Lumet. Sean Connery, Trevor Howard, Vivien Merchant . . . As usual I didn't do it like anyone else would. It's interesting that he [Lumet] let me do what I wanted. It worked out well.

Did you find it hard?

No! I sat down at my desk for two days and wrote a lot of

'wild track' without any relation whatsoever to the film. I'd seen a rough cut. That was all.

There was a series of elements – fragments of chorus, the sound of a child's voice singing, brass chords, lines on single instruments. Then they gave me something called a movieola. You could see the film and run it backwards and forwards. Then in EMS, Peter Zinovieff's Electronic Music Studio, it was all cut together – I did it myself – and manipulated on eight-track by various processes of filtering. So it becomes a collage. I'd learned to do that in *Amadeus* . . . It would be a doddle to do today. Easy. But it was the beginning of computers. And no one interfered and when it was done Lumet just said, 'Terrific.'

It may not be the way film scores were traditionally written then but it sounds in keeping with the processes you've repeatedly described in your own way of working?

The techniques, the mechanics, were different. It was all done in a studio. But the way of thinking, yes, that was similar.

Was The Oresteia *the biggest event at the National? That was an epic piece of theatre, with a lot of music . . .*

Five hours of music. All gone now. Gone.

I said to Peter Hall, I don't want any actors who can read music. It was done with a company of men, even the women's parts. Peter Hall was interested in mask – full masks. The effect is the opposite to the half-mask, which is like *commedia dell'arte*, where the impact is highly physical.

With full masks it immediately makes everything still.

What I didn't want to do was write cosmetic music. In the theatre there is music *of* the play and music *about* the play. The music *about* the play is cosmetic. In simple terms if there's a storm, you make something that sounds like a storm.

On the other hand the music *of* the play is what the actors sing or speak. So a song like 'Full Fathom Five' or Ophelia's song – you have to create music which is of the essence of the play. That's what I wanted to do in *The Oresteia*. I wanted it to be *of* the play. I didn't want it to be external but to relate to the rhythm of the text. So in the end we set every single word. Every word was notated, every pulse.

Tony Harrison's translation was all in iambic pentameters. All I did was write down the rhythm of the text, with certain freedoms to make it more varied.

I wrote a lot of it on the train from Twickenham. The journey to Waterloo took thirty minutes. I could just about write enough stuff to teach the chorus each day . . . but I never mentioned crotchets or quavers. What actors are good at is imitation. So they managed it fine. I worked out a system where there were stops, like a form of punctuation, with gaps – and once they'd learned it I'd say, OK, at this point you wait three beats, or whatever. And somehow we managed it. But the point is it came *out of* the text. We also realised that we couldn't do it in unison. It had to be like a crowd.

Hocketing – your old favourite?

Exactly . . . you say this word, you say that. We designated how it should work.

You have mentioned before the 'Oresteia Pulse Game'?

I invented a lot of exercises for non-musicians including one called the Oresteia Pulse Game – which they had to do because of the discipline of music, which is entirely against what actors do. They sat in a circle. We used cut up broomsticks. They had to pass the pulse. It's a nice game but they didn't take to it. It's against their nature. The essence is this: if someone went click, then you make a space and go click, then the third person has to identify that space and go click. You have to listen.

It was all about changing pulses and listening to rhythm. It's the opposite to the rhythm of pop music. That's probably why they didn't like it at first. It was a routine exercise. But oh, they resisted. Like children. But then they began to understand what it was to speak the text rhythmically.

There was a sense in which Peter Hall, who unlike some directors is exceptionally musical, thought music came out of a packet! He'd say can we have more of this here, now, and I'd say hang on, first I have to write the music, then I have to copy out the parts, then I have to teach it to the musicians . . . When they did *Brand* I recorded hymns from Raasay and the Western Isles.

Jumping back to the 1960s when you were teaching in Wiltshire and Dorset . . . We haven't yet talked about that period. I've always imagined you probably made plays and mini operas with the girls of Cranborne Chase and the prep school boys of Port Regis?

Yes I did a lot of drama there, at Cranborne Chase – and a lot of made-up plays with specially written music for the pupils to play. You should talk to Caroline Mustill, who was there, or Patrick Wright who was at Port Regis. Both are still very close friends . . . they can tell you what we got up to . . .

Fortunately both are willing to co-operate. Caroline Mustill [née Phillips] was a pupil at Cranborne Chase. She learned clarinet with Harry and later, when he decided to concentrate on composition, he sold her his clarinets. She was there during the years of the Wardour Castle Summer School and later, as a university student, helped run the Pierrot Players. Tom Mustill, who featured in a previous conversation, is her son.

CM Cranborne Chase School was first established as a sister school for Bryanston with a similar emphasis on the arts. It was known as 'Crichel' after the beautiful Palladian house which it inhabited, and along with a solid core from the middle classes it drew to it an eclectic mix of daughters of artists and academics, aristocrats and politicians.

   In 1969 Crichel's owner chose not to renew the lease. New Wardour Castle in neighbouring Wiltshire was bought in haste and the school moved there, almost bankrupting itself in the process. Many of the staff left and among their replacements was Harry, alerted by Nicholas Maw to a vacancy for someone to teach clarinet and oboe.

For Harry, that offer, and the cottage that came with it, must have been a godsend. He, Sheila and their small son had been living in Slough in his in-laws' council flat, scraping a living through music-copying and any job he could find in the factories near by.

When he first came to the school, the rumpled figure of Mr Birtwistle caught our attention and aroused our curiosity: sometimes with small son in tow, he would wander along the corridors or around the grand rotunda staircase with his slightly shambling gait, making slow, considered statements in that soft Lancashire accent.

I abandoned my piano lessons and took up the clarinet, and before long Harry sold me his French clarinets. (When I left school, Harry introduced me to Alan Hacker, who, to my regret, insisted that I exchange them for harsher-sounding German ones.) The practice rooms where we had our lessons were at the top of the East Wing, but Harry was rarely to be found there. Instead he haunted the art and sculpture rooms, or the pottery. On an outside wall at their house in Mere there is a long, clay face, a sort of Green Man, which he made there. A friend, Serena Macintosh Walker, remembered him as 'perceptive, different'. Arriving one day for her lesson, she tracked him down to the art room, where he was lying on a bench. 'I don't think I can teach you today, you are far too angry to play the clarinet,' he said, at which she flounced out, slamming the door behind her, only to have the doorknob come off in her hand. I, too, remember turning up for my lesson in tears – some perceived injustice on the tennis court – and that's

[CM] what we spent the lesson talking about. Later, when I told Harry I was going to read Chinese at university, I recall him saying, 'If it were me, I'd want to learn about my own culture first.' As Cat Mackintosh said when I asked her for her recollections: 'We all loved Harry, not necessarily because of the music, but because he was a very sympathetic person who took us seriously.'

When we took our Grade 5 Theory, Harry hovered behind us with a box of Cadbury's Milk Tray, and when he saw that we had enough marks to pass, we were allowed to take a chocolate and depart. His methods may have been 'unorthodox', as another former pupil, Dinah Casson, described them, but music nevertheless was important. In addition to the traditional clarinet repertoire for solo instrument and wind ensembles he made arrangements of ancient music and introduced us to new composers. I'll never forget a performance of Ives's *Unanswered Question* with players placed in recesses around the rotunda, likewise a lecture he gave on Messiaen. Introduced to Boulez's music by Harry, I played a record of *Le Marteau sans maître* until it had become so familiar that a performance heard many years later with far fewer wrong notes was deeply disconcerting. Then there was *The Green Man*, *Noe* and *The Seven Simeons*, productions with masks and mime for which he composed music for us to play. Harry was less enthusiastic when required to take part in staff performances. My sister Jane remembers a pantomime in which Harry, with wings on his head and no attempt at acting, said 'I'm Mercury. This is the West Wing and this is the East Wing', gesturing each time in the wrong direction. It brought the house down.

To a strictly brought-up teenager Harry's and Sheila's way of life was sheer delight. Invited, first, to a Sunday lunch of boiled eggs and apple pie, which we ate on our knees in front of the fire with small boys running round, I was soon spending half-terms and much of the holidays with them. Chickens in the bath and nappies on the stairs, icy bedrooms and an ancient iron that Sheila heated on the stove, all formed part of the enchantment. The poverty, at least to me, went unnoticed. Their easy hospitality meant the house was full of friends: their lodger, John Telford, and his friend Michael Nyman, both students at the Royal Academy of Music, rented a shack in the woods above the old castle. Max [Peter Maxwell Davies], with his intense and often unsettling gaze, soon bought a house near by. There was Noah Morris, a local sculptor whose wife taught us French, and Robin Yapp, a dentist before he turned to importing wine. The lack of money never seemed to prevent them from eating well. Harry had a kitchen garden and would come in with his arms full of vegetables. I remember him holding out some potatoes he'd dug up: 'Look at these!' he said, and the potatoes, with the black soil still clinging to them, were suddenly mysterious, objects of wonder.

The year I left school Harry hatched a plan he had had in his head for some time. Together with Sandy [Alexander Goehr] and Max (and with Cat Mackintosh's mother as unpaid administrator), he set up a summer

[CM] school of music at Wardour, first imagined as a sort of English Darmstadt, which was repeated the following year. It was there that *Tragoedia* had its first performance.

Embarking on my Chinese degree in London, I readily accepted Harry's request to 'run' the Pierrot Players, a group set up to perform music composed by him and his friends, while he and Sheila were in America. With Steve Pruslin in his basement flat beneath a run-down shop in Camden Passage and my student flat above it, a new era had begun.

Patrick Wright, Professor of Literature and Visual and Material Culture at King's College, University of London, has written about Harry and also interviewed him in various television and radio documentaries. His essay 'On Melancholy and the Humour of the Night', a discussion of Birtwistle's music and Dürer's engraving *Melencolia I* (1514), is included in the programme book for Roche Commissions: *Sir Harrison Birtwistle* (2004). Along with a further essay, entitled 'Facing up to the Subterranean Stream' and dealing with Robin Blaser's libretto for *The Last Supper*, it is available on the Boosey & Hawkes website.

Wright first encountered Harry when he was a nine-year-old preparatory school pupil at Port Regis School in Blackmore Vale, Dorset, in or shortly after 1960. Harry was an instrumental teacher and Wright learned the flute.

PW Harry seemed to arrive from another world. He was a young Lancastrian who certainly seemed different in that South of England upper middle-class environment, and he was introduced as a composer rather than a teacher. The headmaster of Port Regis was John Upward, whose brother Edward was a friend of Auden and Isherwood and a novelist whose life – like some of his novels – combined schoolmastering with devotion to the Communist Party. I remember the austerity, a sharp sense of class separation and occasional signs of liberal idealism, not least in the headmaster's habit of allowing boys to watch approved TV programmes on the black-and-white set in his study, including, if I remember rightly, the first run of *Doctor Who*. The school was in a rather gaunt late-Victorian mansion situated among woods filled with boys playing games like 'French and English', and building tree houses with the help of penknives and old school counterpanes. It was the kind of place, as Harry once reminded me, where you could learn how to tie salmon flies but never go fishing. And it was all set in deep English countryside with only an occasional train hauling itself through the vale to indicate the wider life beyond.

Harry was part-time and peripatetic and I don't think he really wanted to be there. He needed somewhere to live at that time – he'd got the Cranborne Chase job – and John Upward allowed him to live in Upper Lodge House, at the end of the drive, in return for a bit of music teaching. Nowadays the school feels moneyed – very well equipped and decidedly up-market. I guess it's not been the same since Princess Anne sent her children there. In the early 1960s, however, there was still a lot of rusty wire about and some of the fields outside the main building were full of abandoned Nissen-like buildings which had been used to house Italian prisoners during the Second World War. I remember one that still had the word 'Ablutions' stencilled on the door.

Some of the teachers might have dropped out of the pages of a John Le Carré novel, and the educational ethos was pretty distinctive too. Port Regis was a feeder school for Bryanston, where the founding headmaster Thorold Coade had preached that life was not a race but a dance. Music was certainly given some priority at Port Regis. It was compulsory for everyone to learn the violin, taught in largely reluctant groups by a teacher named Miss Dalrymple. Poor woman! I remember her as a fright, and impossibly elderly, though she probably wasn't. The violins were kept piled up in a big trunk at the back of the room. We played pizzicato for what may really have been years before we were eventually allowed to try out a bow. There was a lot of fooling about and the sounds were terrible. I later discussed the set-up with Harry. He remembered coming along the corridor on one of his first visits and, as he approached the classroom, hearing Miss Dalrymple roaring out: 'Move that flesh, move that flesh'!

Harry's arrival was surely greeted with a sense of relief as well as puzzlement. He was not like any other teacher I'd met – his informal clothes, the fact he didn't shave all that regularly – I imagine he was probably up all night composing *Punch and Judy*. He obviously wasn't looking to make friends with the pupils, but he was also impressively indifferent to the idea that he might be expected to serve as a disciplined role model . . . I can remember Sheila and the boys tumbling around at the lodge and it all looked curiously encouraging – proof that there were various ways of living your life. I think he had more or less given up playing the clarinet by that stage, but he certainly taught it. He was also tolerant of the incompetent and irregular noises I produced in my attempts to play the flute.

When it came to performances, he turned the musical ethos of the school upside down. It was all rather wild and exciting. As I recall, Harry would write music for whatever instruments he had at his disposal. People who would never previously have been allowed to stand up and play at concerts found themselves doing just that. As long as you could play three notes, he'd write a part for you, and you would end up performing in a scratch ensemble that, for pretty obvious reasons, included quite a lot of simple percussion and, in some cases, I think, also girls from another school at which he taught. It was completely other than anything I had experienced before. It could be uncomfortable but it was great to see how music could be made – that it had a sociability and drama about it and was not just a matter of staggering along in individual contest with the grades. I never did become an even half-able flautist, but that early experience gave me a strong and, as I later found, quite transferable sense of what form and the process of composition could and should be.

Of course I moved on and Harry soon went off on his fellowship to the States. I didn't meet him again for

[PW] three decades but I kept an ear open for his music. I remember being much taken with that wonderful piece *Fields of Sorrow*, with its octaves of slightly denatured Es, and *Nenia: The Death of Orpheus* and *Triumph of Time* too. I guess I have always been aware of him as representative of an independent way of life that few can manage to get away with, deeply engaged with issues of form and tradition but not bound by formulaic rules, and in this sense a model of the best kind of twentieth-century creativity – one that invents its own conditions of existence in a constantly changing conversation with the past. Of course I also admired his persistence and the stories I sometimes heard of the risks he had taken and the battles he had fought in defence of his music.

In some respects he's like a maker or craftsman, with a grounded outlook connected to his material and tradition, but he's got a wonderful intellectual reach too. This is not a general matter of knowing a lot about art or cinema, or being 'well read' in the conventional sense of having ploughed through a lot of texts. It is quite different to hear Harry thinking along with the books, films and images that speak to him at particular times – David Sylvester on Bacon, Sebald, Cees Nooteboom's *Road to Santiago* . . . I've always been fascinated by the way he uses visual images to describe and perhaps structure and guide his compositions. There is, for example, quite a lot of landscape in the background of the music – *Silbury Air*, *Earth Dances*, etc. – but it's hardly a descriptive presence or a mimicry of larks ascending, for example, or of someone striding over Egdon Heath. The influence is surely far more molten and geological, and deeper in the compositional process.

I got a clearer sense of that after we met up again in the 1990s. I was then writing for the *Guardian*, and I went to see him at Lunegarde in France.

By then we happened to have another place in common. Through the 1960s my parents had a former crofter's cottage on the mainland of Scotland opposite Raasay. Having got to know that coast and the Inner Hebridean islands quite well, I was interested to hear of his time there. I had seen the amazing view he looked out over from his composing shed – or was it a 'pod'? – near the water's edge, and I was also aware of Sorley Maclean, the Raasay-born Gaelic poet who had been headmaster of the school at Plockton, where children from across a wide area used to board during the week and learn Gaelic with, as I recall, varying degrees of enthusiasm. I knew about the ongoing trials of the big house on Raasay, grievously neglected by the island's absentee owner, a Sussex doctor named Green who is said only ever to have gone to the place once. Indeed, in the late 1960s people were apparently going over to Raasay House and carrying off boatloads of books from the library, which had been in place when James Boswell and Samuel Johnson stayed there in 1773.

Green was the most negligent of owners, and Harry was among those who took care of some of the increasingly derelict house's furniture. Indeed, I think he would have been sued for his efforts had Green not died

[PW] before he got to court. There is, by the way, a wonderful account of Harry's own departure from the island and of the gap he left in the mind of his neighbour: it's in Timothy Neat's book *When I Was Young: Voices from Lost Communities in Scotland* and it comes from Donald Macleod, who for years lived next to Harry at Eyre on the south of the island. Having heard that Harry had exchanged his marvellous view over mountain and water for a 'planted hedge' somewhere in France, he remembers Harry saying, '"Having looked on the Cuillin, I know nothing can match them. My going from here is like a bereavement – but Raasay is still there in my music, as much as my parents are here in my hand." And that was it, we haven't seen him since.' In 2008 we took Timothy Neat's film *Hallaig*, about Sorley Maclean and Raasay, to Aldeburgh, and showed it as an accompaniment to the first performance of Harry's string quartet, *Tree of Strings*.

On that visit to Lunegarde we also talked a lot about Harry's long-standing interest in Dürer's *Melencolia I* – an engraving which has long preoccupied him for its enigmatic balance of contraries. It depicts a seated angel, winged but immobile and surely far too heavy to fly. This famously dark-visaged figure is resting in some sort of building site full of tools and instruments that have been laid to rest. Everything suggests movement and activity, but at the same time everything is still. Stasis in mobility, and vice versa, as Günter Grass described it in *From the Diary of a Snail*, one of the many texts Harry has read in his exploration of this theme. When

[96]

you think of this, and the various ways in which Harry works with ancient musical materials from Dowland and others, you are likely to get more amazed at the ignorance of the idea, still occasionally put about by rock-music journalists on BBC arts programmes, that he is some kind of transgressive, avant-garde, Year-Zero nihilist. Nothing could be further from the truth. A great deal of his music seems to me to be closely engaged with considerations of inheritance, discontinuity and descent, and fully aware of its participation in the passage of time . . .

You can see this in his engagement with the ancient and yet ongoing tradition of Melancholia. It may be that Harry has a slightly depressive turn in this ancient 'humour of the night'. I am sure he knows about insomnia and what it can do to one's daytime sense of measure. But he also does extraordinary formal things with the melancholy perspective. It was intriguing, at the premiere of *Night's Black Bird* in Lucerne, to talk about this with the scientists at Roche – the company, after all, which is responsible for Valium! In *Melencolia I*, for example, he uses the sharp difference between clarinets and strings as a compositional principle which is like the play of contrasts between black and white in an engraving. He then takes the sense of repetition, circularity, disconnection and suspension – which are all long-standing characteristics of melancholy thought – of 'melancholising' as practised by Burton [*The Anatomy of Melancholy, 1621*] and of course of John Dowland and Shakespeare too. Going back to Dürer's

[PW] heavy and immobilised angel, it is surely very touching that Harry wrote *Melencolia I* around the time Alan Hacker was becoming paraplegic. I believe he dedicated the piece to Hacker, but the idea of the immobilised angel is absolutely central to the composition of the music too.

Later we hooked up again, this time with the West Coast poet Robin Blaser, librettist of *The Last Supper* – I had studied with Robin as a postgraduate student in Canada during the 1970s. Blaser was interested in music as well as in the Orphic tradition with its ideas of descent into the underworld – and at some point I'd given him a copy of the old Decca LP with *Death of Orpheus* and *Fields of Sorrow* on it. So it was nice later to be able to do things the other way round. I suppose the first thing Harry gleaned from Robin was the word 'Exody', a more or less obsolete term with Old Testament resonances, which Robin had revived as the title of a group of poems he'd written in the early 1990s. Blaser's 'exody' is much concerned with movement, journeying forward, transcending – or perhaps not – various bad forms of power, religion and politics. I guess it was also about passing through an often highly oppressive and disturbing history in a way that still bears testimony to its shape. Robin was amused by the use made of the word by a Victorian writer, George MacDonald – he'd found it in the *Oxford English Dictionary* – who had spoken of 'the plomp of the cork's exody, and the gurgle of the wine'! It was at about the same time that Harry mentioned he was looking for a writer who could bring something new and interesting – a kind of critical archaeology as well as a narrative – to a work looking back at the Last Supper through two millennia of Christian history in the year 2000. We all met up in Chicago in February 1998, using the Chicago Symphony Orchestra's premiere of Harry's *Exody* as an opportunity to spend a few winter days launching the collaboration that produced *The Last Supper*.

9 May 2013

WILTSHIRE. SPIKES OF BRIGHT SUNLIGHT PIERCE THE LENGTH OF THE HOUSE. THE STRONG WIND IS FROM THE SOUTH. TEMPERATURE 13 DEGREES.

Harry comes to the door. 'I'm high.' This is evidently a psychological, not a chemically induced state. Pots of yellow narcissi, placed near the French windows, cheer up a garden that is otherwise still bare. The young gingko is creeping slowly into leaf. The man who mows the lawn has come to mow the lawn. Harry has baked large, round digestive biscuits, stored in a glass jar. They look like thick, oversized oatcakes.

He directs me to get milk from the fridge. On a shelf, unwrapped, is what looks like a big slab of old yellow cheese. It is not cheese. 'Pig's cheek. Delicious, you know?' Harry retrieves it and holds it against his ear to show the unmistakable porcine jawline. 'Don't forget my father was a pig farmer.

We had hundreds of little pigs.' He chuckles. The 'noises off' on the recording today are the sounds of hard, crunched biscuits. Unusually, Harry launches straight into conversation.

The pianist is playing [Messiaen's] *Oiseaux exotiques* in the concert –

You mean in the concert at which the new piano concerto will be played?

Yes. I feel I could push the idea – do I mean plagiarise? No. I mean make a dense bed of strings, like a canvas – I got a glimpse of something in *The Minotaur* where, near the beginning, the flute plays something on its own, over this bed of strings, and it's quite intimate.

The idea was very clear to me. I've often done that. You hear a corner of something, you stumble on it and you think, I could do something with that. And I've no idea why I did that bit in *The Minotaur* but it really worked.

Does it come anywhere else in the opera?

No, just for those two or three seconds. And on what I'm calling this bed of sound the flute solo is very clearly etched. I could certainly do – well, I haven't done it yet, so I don't know – but I think I could move from something which is very fluid, and birdlike – I wouldn't try to imitate any birds; I'd just invent them myself – and I could make them become mechanical, yes? It would have to come at the end, when you have a mellifluous passage – this is purely conceptual, Fiona.

I have no idea whether it will turn out like this. I'm telling you what's in my head. It would dissolve into mechanistics – now that's a clear image, isn't it? It might be a way of ending it. I've never thought of anything before which tries to plagiarise something – or make something which is derived from something else.

Pays homage to? Rather than plagiarise (since apart from anything you are acknowledging the borrowing which plagiarism doesn't)?

Maybe. Like a lot of words one uses it might be the wrong one. What's more interesting is that in the context of this piece, the relationship is certainly going to be heard. I don't know whether the Messiaen will be performed first. The connection will be there. It will be audible, noticeable. The critics will hear it, what? Give them something to write about . . . [*Laughter.*] Maybe. [*More laughter.*]

Will you tell them?

No. I won't tell anybody. I feel it's a homage. I'm not trying to send it up, or imitate it. It's a big reference. It's not a quote. You make it for yourself. There are certain techniques in old music I've used but this is more specific.

The thing about birdsong when you hear it, it has a clear identification, yet it's mellifluous within the context of a dawn chorus. But it's identifiable too: you can identify the birds within it.

So you're saying you can, even if you decide otherwise, see where this piano concerto is heading, even though you say that's not usually how you think about what you're writing?

Yes. My mind's moving ahead. I'm seeing how I can make the piano retain its supremacy within the orchestral context. So we'll see. That's all I can say. But there's something about knowing completely about something yet being ignorant about it. I lived for nearly ten years looking at the sea, in Scotland. And of course you see most sea birds at a distance. There's as much identification from a distance as close because you never see them close. You buy a bird book and you never get an opportunity to see them as they show you in the pictures. For instance those millions of starlings – most people think, oh, they're just black birds, but they're the most extraordinarily beautiful things, bronzed, speckled, shiny. Because they're always associated with being in a flock, you just take them for granted.

From where I sat gazing out at sea I began to identify certain birds from their physical characteristics. I was particularly interested in the divers. There's a red-throated diver and a great northern diver. You can see the diving action from a distance, but you never get near enough to see which is which. I think that I worked out – or I like to think I did – that by timing their diving patterns and the amount of time they were under the water, I could tell one from another. The great northern diver spent longer under. I had a chart of the timings.

I also found that if they're big birds and you can follow their wing beats, even at a great distance, you can learn a lot.

By putting the metronome on to them [their wing beats] you can see that birds don't seem to fly faster or slower . . .

So you see a parallel in the way you know what a new piece will be like without in some senses knowing anything?

Yes. Exactly.

It's the same kind of thing with people who go on that TV quiz *Mastermind*. They have to walk to and from that chair twice. You can tell so much about how they walk, where they put their arms, that kind of thing. Extraordinary. You glean so much information from those walks. Actors are taught to do that sort of thing but the rest of us can't. I remember when I first went to the National. In *Tamburlaine* I had two percussion ensembles, and there were two gates on the stage.

I said to Peter Hall, 'Wouldn't it be wonderful if the players could walk through those gates and then begin to play?' Peter and I sat in the stalls with everything ready – the lights, the doors ready to open and close . . . There were six of them. Three on each side. They got halfway down the Olivier stage and Peter said, 'Cut!' They couldn't walk properly. They just couldn't! It was hopeless. We abandoned the idea . . . [*Chuckles.*]

We decided last time that on future occasions we would talk about the progress you've been making with the piano concerto – a quick update. Last time you were stuck . . .

Stuck? Was I stuck?

You probably can't remember . . . Maybe you resolved it.

I can't remember. I'm always stuck. My neurosis is that being something of a somnambulist – no, that's when you get out of bed, isn't it? – I mean being something of an insomniac, my neurosis is that I move into a kind of half sleep, trying to solve the problem – which I never ever do. I know I'm not telling you anything you wouldn't already know – no doubt everyone tries to do the same – but the interesting thing is that the problem sort of becomes clear.

What I think I'm doing as I walk through the door to my desk the next morning – I did that today – is that I sit at my desk and do the first thing that comes into my head, and that feels real. But it's nothing to do with my night thoughts. I don't refer to my neurotic state. Again it is possible that because I do think of something – I suppose you would say, an idea – as I go through the door in the morning, my subconscious has been sorting it out. That's what I think.

How much have you written in the past week?

I'm on page 20. I was on page 15 before.

And you've got to get to page 28 before you go to Japan in a few days?

Is that what I said?

Yes.

Well, I'm not going to. But I feel all right about it.

But some pages are denser than others...

They're all dense . . . ! Well, no, they're not, but God, the ones I've just done are pretty dense. If I can write three pages a week I'm doing OK. Did I tell you what happened about my guitar piece?

That the guitarist you've written it for edited it and that Julian [Bream] had said he didn't absolutely understand it.

Anyway this American guitarist said it's all playable.

Is it, do you think, like athletes beating ever faster records – instrumentalists overcoming ever harder technical challenges?

I don't know. But the idea was that he encouraged me to write it without thinking too much about the idiom or technique of the instrument. But I did. I made a chart where your fingers go.

You can see why it's complex. If you have a violin piece, you don't play chords across all the strings except maybe one or two. But with the guitar it's the whole technique of the instrument. And the problem is, if you play one note and you move, you've lost it. It's not like a piano. If you play a chord on the piano you can hold it through and play another chord. But with a guitar if you move to the next chord, the last one doesn't exist. You've lost it. That's the fundamental problem of the instrument.

[105]

That's why I can write for the harp, or violin or whatever. But because the guitar is a harmonic instrument, moving in blocks, to write contrapuntal music for it needs very careful handling – so it ends up in one or two parts. Anyway, he says it's playable – by and large.

[He makes tea – white porcelain beakers on a tray, a Japanese green tea definitely not available at your local supermarket.]

It's very civilised. Looks like soggy lettuce, doesn't it? You stuff it down and leave it. Some people apparently drink it all day . . . non-stop. I've seen it in hotels. 'Old' folk. [*Chuckles.*]

So going back to how you work, keeping up the momentum is crucial? You say you can do three pages a week.

It's just a way of thinking about it. It's how I usually work. I have a sort of length – I can't write movements. I've never written movements. I've written pieces, unless it's a song text then you stop at the end of the song. It's just a lot of bits stuck together, my music!

It's certainly what you keep saying.

It is! The great piece for me which, apart from being a wonderful piece, got me out of a lot of problems, was Stravinsky's *Symphonies of Wind Instruments*, which is one of my favourite pieces. In one way it's a bad model. It just does one thing and then another. But it made it possible for me to avoid certain problems – concerning what they call the bridge passage in music.

You mean as in sonata form?

Were you taught all that stuff? 'Bridge passage in Beethoven'
and all that? The idea of doing something then going to
something else . . . Well, I did begin to devise ways of not
letting the process be simply a kind of musical cubism – ways
of getting from one part to another, and it not being just bits
rubbed up next to each other.

How did you avoid that?

Just *did* it.

Yes, but how?

Have we talked about repetition? Have we talked about how
you get out of something, how you move on from material?
You can just stop it and do something else. This is one of the
most important things. We've got to talk about it. It means
a lot. It means a big lump.

   It comes from Paul Klee. He talks about 'dividual' and
'individual'.

Meaning?

Wallpaper is dividual, OK? Meaning if you take a piece out
of it, it retains its formal quality. It comes by the yard. Liquid
is the same. You can take a drop of wine and it's still the same
wine in the bottle.

The phone rings. It's the guitarist, Jonathan Leathwood – Harry's first conversation with him. 'Oh hello. Great . . . I'm glad you like my piece . . . Can you come round? We'll go through it. You can tell me how to make it better?' He ends the call. 'He said it was the best new guitar piece in the last twenty years!' He is chuckling, pleased at the idea rather than really believing it. Soon after he makes a call. 'Julian? Jonathan Leathwood says it's the best piece in fifty years . . !'

10 May 2013

WILTSHIRE. THE COLD HAS RETURNED. A GUSTY WEST WIND DISTURBS THE TREES BUT THERE ARE GLIMPSES OF SUN AFTER RAIN. TEMPERATURE 12 DEGREES.

The young gingko is now in full leaf. Ferns unfurl. A man who prunes trees has come to prune the mature pear tree in the middle of the lawn. He is not the man who mows the lawn. He has, however, been to work for Harry before. 'When he first came I knew he was religious,' Harry says, without elaborating. The man has dark hair with streaks of silver, a handsome, weather-tanned chiselled face. He and Harry discuss an old quince tree whose bark has split and whose future is doubtful. The tree man, who has a friendly, intelligent manner, wears no obvious badges of faith. And was Harry right? Was the man religious? 'Oh yes. Very,' Harry says. How did he know? 'I asked him.'

You said yesterday when you were showing me what you'd just written that you realised that you'd made a specific mistake — copied something wrong, I think. Did you sort it out?

It's very simple. It's a technical error. Honestly, it's stupid. I had to rub the whole thing out. I was trying to divide the strings. I need to make the balance of the upper strings, divided into four – but there are only three sections, first and second violins and viola. So some of the seconds had to straddle the violas. That's all it was. When you came through the door, I saw what I'd done wrong and how to make it work in a much simpler way.

Which is basically what?

This is not interesting, but I started by dividing the violas into two. But then I realised the first half of the violas are in the violin range, so I could take that out and move it all around . . .

But it'll still be two-thirds violins, one-third violas?

It's terribly boring I'm afraid. In order to solve it I didn't go far enough back [in the score]. When you've gone I'll go back and rub it all out and what's taken me all morning to puzzle over I'll sort out in half an hour.

This one I've just done is a hell of a page . . . Anyway . . .

Is it like recalibrating something, then?

Yes. You've got to go back again. I see orchestration as a problem of balance. I mean what's the difference between forte on a high trumpet and forte on a single violin? I've said that before. If you could weigh them, they'd be different.

If you write something down you need it to be heard. But in a way I deal in perspective, the whole idea of what is foreground, middle, background in music. I'm very conscious of that all the time. I don't orchestrate from a piano reduction. I write music rather as a process of adding things. I don't write anything where I don't try to hear the instrument. It's not abstract, in which I think: wouldn't it be interesting to put this with this, wouldn't it be interesting to play this on the oboe? It's for the instrument. There's no formula.

It's quite clear, marvellous though it is, that someone like Wagner had a formula for orchestration. He must have done some of it very, very quickly, and he did it wonderfully.

Can you give an example of what you mean in Wagner?

I think it's sort of fixed, what the role of the strings are and how the brass works, and it never really varies all that much. But it's wonderfully heard. I think his use of wanting more horns, for instance, in the form of Wagner tubas, is all a question of balance, of needing an equality in the orchestra, not provided from, say, three trombones in the standard orchestra.

Not to go through a whole list of composers –

Why not?

OK, Verdi. Think of that moment in Don Carlos *when the Grand Inquisitor enters and there's all that low woodwind, bassoons and double bassoons . . .*

It's sort of similar. I'll bet – I don't know, I'm just speaking from the experience of trying to do it myself – it's what is traditionally called orchestration. Do you know he used to stand in a pit, Verdi, with a bass drum and play the whole of it, banging it out, and saying this is forte, and they sang to it. We're touching on a lot of things here.

I'm very self-conscious about what I do . . . and I'm not good at talking about it, if it is even necessary to talk about it . . . I'm going through a bad minute here.

This bit here [*points to where he is up to in the score*], it's a question of trying to do something that's in layers, yes? One of the characteristics of music is, say if you take something like counterpoint, what do you actually hear? You can't hear all the things that are going on. For example it's hard to tell the difference between four and five parts. I think three is as many as you can hear. Apart from people with big ears. You know, there are people with big ears who can hear everything . . .

So I'm very interested that when you have simultaneous music, even in parts that are contrapuntal, you don't really hear four parts, you hear another one-ness, an accumulation of things.

So this here [*referring to score*] is an attempt to do something . . . there's no solo piano here. It's an orchestral tutti.

The other day we were talking about that painter, who painted and his wife painted and they were very similar.

Robert and Sonia Delaunay?

Yes, Delaunay. They used very basic colours against each other. I don't know how to explain this. It's an attempt to write something which is a tutti but at the same time the ingredients of the tutti are individual. That means that the colours are individual.

I know that would seem, in some people's minds, the most obvious thing to do. Sometimes you have to have the right to be simple. You earn the right to be simple. There's a very self-conscious attempt to do it, simply, in the layers of materials: here, for example [*refers to score*], percussion doing that, trumpets and horns doing something else, woodwind doing something else, lower strings doing something else, then upper strings that I was dealing with this morning doing something else again. So for a couple of pages there are these individual strands of colour if you like. If I hadn't taken such a radical move to use these basic colours, I wouldn't be able to achieve the independence of the layers. Do you understand what I'm saying?

When you say radical . . .

Well, I consider it radical. Something absolutely stark. First of all there's a question of a register. There's one layer that is low. I'm just thinking pitch-wise. There's one that has wooden instruments. There's another layer that is muted brass. But I'm trying to relate two layers – percussion, that you'll hear very clearly, the other is the muted brass.

But the attacks of the brass and the percussion never occur at the same time, yes?

Look at it [*pointing at score*]: they never double the rhythmical world. That demisemiquaver – the de-*donk* – happens here, but this one plays after it – de-*donk*, de-*donk*. I've characterised it by doing it in two different colours – the muted brass and the percussion.

And even within the brass there's an interdependency. There's another rhythm going on within that. It's not just a question of doubling things. They all have individuality, everything moving on its own.

Something happens here, there's a sudden woodwind chorus and it's always the same thing, getting closer together – can you see? [*pointing to high woodwind*] – so the music tempo is the same but the space between each bit of action is getting shorter. And it's not just a question of doubling everything . . .

So the whole thing is becoming denser?

. . . until here, this chord, is four notes and eight instruments, then it doubles. Then it explodes into eight parts. Pairs divide and there's an intensification. So there's a logic to the journey. Here, all these down-beats, where they were never in the same place, they're all together. They're all playing a doubling of the down-beat but they have independent rhythms to each other apart from the down-beat. I can draw it for you. [*Draws several long lines interrupted by a shorter.*] Everything retains its individuality.

[113]

The piano has been silent for, maybe, twenty-five seconds. I'm attempting to set up the entry of the piano again, as much as other musical reasons. That's what I'm thinking of. It's all about setting up the dialogue with the piano. That's particularly what the piece is about. Maybe all concertos are about dialogue. But traditionally in a classical concerto they are sharing the same material. I'll play a bit of the tune then you'll do a bit. Beethoven is very good at that. In the Violin Concerto the violin takes a long time to enter then it comes in accompanying the orchestra. It's a long time until the violin has its own material.

I used to tell students that. Discuss the role of the violin in Beethoven's concerto. It's not like Mozart: you play, I play.

And how is it in relation to what came later? Brahms? Mendelssohn?

I don't really know. Can't remember. I haven't thought about that. I've just thought about the Beethoven and I didn't really hear it like that until a few years ago . . .

What about the other concerto tradition of combat, between soloist and orchestra?

I don't like the idea of combat. The piano is an ingredient. It's an equal thing. They may both have material that doesn't belong to the other but none of what happens is proscribed or prescribed. But it's not an argument between piano and orchestra. More protagonist and chorus.

And this sense of rhythmic individuality you're describing, can you create it in microcosm within the piano part, with the action of the ten fingers?

Oh yes, definitely. Or in the guitar piece I've just done. You look at some of that. See this part [*finds a section in the guitar piece*], these three notes are always the same, but the upper part is independent to it. You could say, well that's just what accompaniment is. But it's not. It's not reflecting what is in the upper part. It's *obstinately* against it. So I don't change these three notes, they're always the same, yeah? Does that make sense?

So to express that plainly, it's always the same three notes in the bass . . . and the top is doing its own thing?

Yes. I'm creating an independency. The parts don't mesh. They remain whole. It's like a permanent state of collision.

But nothing is destroyed in the collision? The elements stop, intact, at the point they meet each other?

That's right. Nothing is destroyed. I could easily have done that. If I'd have moved that sort of ostinato figure in order to make it work with what's above, it would have turned into a standard ostinato accompaniment. But it's as if the upper part starts moving away and the lower part has an obstinacy, against what is above it which defines its independence. OK?

This seems to be getting close to your Klee ideas of dividual and individual?

Yes. It's like the liquid and the bottle again. One's the liquid and one's the bottle. If you change the quantity, the quantity itself becomes individual though the liquid stays the same . . . The taste of mild is constant but a pint or three-quarters of a pint is different. Now we're really hitting on something, though I'm very conscious of stating the obvious. It's like tapestry in a way . . .

Just a minute . . .

[He breaks off at this key point of revelation to say hello to the Polish cleaner. The point we were 'hitting on' has gone by the time he returns.]

I was arranging some arias from Bach cantatas. I listened to hundreds of arias. I sort of knew them and didn't know them. They had to have certain ingredients – a soprano, an oboe – that were in the forces I was writing for, so that cut it right down.

And here's a statement of the obvious. It occurred to me that the music of that period, and before, is about gesture. Whatever the gesture is applies to the whole movement. If you listen to a Bach aria, in a sense it's all surprise. Yet he sets up the gesture and carries it through the entire piece.

The dramatic ingredient is very cubist. You can tell immediately how the piece is going to be at the start and it won't change unless there's a sudden change in the text. You can disagree with me . . .

So where does the element of surprise come in?

[116]

It doesn't. It's all surprise. It's the same with Machaut or whoever. But it does at the end what it's set up at the beginning. In essence it's like itself all the way through. You can tell from the ingredients that there's not suddenly going to be a totally different element in the middle of that three-minute piece or whatever it is. You don't listen to Bach and think, oh, that's a good bit . . .

Well hang on, yes, you do . . . the middle of Wachet auf at the Alleluia when it changes mood. Or the middle of the Chaconne. Or others.

Maybe gesture is the wrong word. All the elements within.

[He starts singing the opening of the Double Violin Concerto, first the second violin entry then the first.]

You see you know where it's going . . .

Are you saying it's not interesting?

No, I'm saying it's *all* interesting. It's all good. What makes it good is something that happens in the first two bars and goes all the way through. You listen to a mass of Byrd, three-part, five-part . . . the same thing is happening.

You can't say that about the Beethoven Violin Concerto. Or the use of the bassoon in the Fourth Symphony. Go and listen to it.

Beethoven recognised something in the Fourth Symphony. I used to think he recognised a lyrical quality in the bassoon

[117]

which no one had before. Until, that is, I heard the slow movement of the Mozart Bassoon Concerto. It's one of the great mezzo arias in music.

And it's very early too. It's all there: the aria in Mozart.

The relationship between the solo bassoon and the tutti is all there too, as it is in the music I used to play – the [Mozart] Clarinet Quintet or Clarinet Concerto. They're almost recompositions of the same tune.

Coming back to Beethoven, as we keep seeming to, would you say that in Fidelio *the way the orchestra is used defies all usual conventions of solo and tutti, aria and accompaniment?*

Yes. I've always thought that about *Fidelio*. It's the odd one out. But then he was the odd one out.

I'm edging towards this very simple concept – as in the Paul Klee I've referred to before, and in Stravinsky's *Symphonies of Wind Instruments* –

We began to discuss that. You said that piece, in effect, saved your creative life.

– it's very hard to know how to talk about these things. It gives the wrong impression if one were to think that all I did was listen to the *Symphonies of Wind Instruments* where he doesn't have any bridge passages and he simply goes from one thing to another and so I thought oh I can do that too . . . It's not like that. I like to think there was a genuine identification.

Like the thing I was talking to you about before – the *Symphonies of Wind* could not have been written if he'd taken a more subtle method. It had to be as radical as that. One thing doesn't just lead to another.

So it ties in with your chopping up material and fitting it together again?

Exactly. Something like this – the piano concerto – is very much like that. Like bricks in a wall.

But it's not just: here's the end of the wall, let's build a new one. Every chord, every element, is setting up what's coming next or reflecting what has gone before. I could have just plonked it all down anywhere. But they are all strands, coming together. In some respects it all seems obvious, a very simple concept, but I think you earn the right to become simple. I've battled with this notion a lot. I could easily have set up a smokescreen and you wouldn't hear it. It has to be something absolutely severely layered for it to do what it has to do.

So what would constitute a smokescreen in this context?

What would constitute a smokescreen? Trying to relate the ideas in some way, or be more impressionistic and cloud the issues in some way. I know that in order to achieve what I want I have to do something severe for it to be what I want it to be.

Do you think your music is ever impressionistic?

No. Never. I'd like to be able to. But I can't.

When people talk about Debussy as impressionistic –

You mean wispy? I can be wispy!

– you see common ground in the way his music and yours works?

In Debussy the impressionistic effect comes in the harmony. I heard a performance of the *Préludes* a while ago and – I think it was the pianist's playing, I hope it was – it all sounded like the same piece, you know? I couldn't differentiate one from another. Because the whole-tone scale only has six notes, it becomes more static for that reason.

But this [*points to the section we have talked about*] is a static concept, but I built into it certain elements that have motion – the idea of this section moving and becoming denser.

It's a question of rhythm and pulse too. We have to talk about those. If you take the famous bars of the opening of the second section of *The Rite of Spring*, it's the same chord. [*He picks out a chord on the electronic keyboard.*] And what do the accents do? They draw attention to the repetition.

It's quite possible that everything I'm doing comes from those few bars of Stravinsky, who knows?

It makes something that is dividual – the repeated chords, the same all the way through – become individual. That's what the accents do. When you throw a pebble into the water that's the element of surprise.

You have often spoken of Debussy's Jeux *as an important piece in your life. Is it significant for any of the same reasons we've been discussing?*

Yes and no. What's remarkable about *Jeux* is that in that piece he never does what you expect him to do. It makes it very modern.

So really what you are talking about is modernism?

Yes. Modernism is indeed what we're talking about. Beethoven and modernism: discuss.

I'm talking about gestures. In *Secret Theatre* there are gestures that repeat and repeat and repeat. But if you examine them, they're never the same. I systematically worked it out. It comes from a way of thinking, which I like to believe I learned from that book we were looking at [*Nature's Numbers* by Ian Stewart] – the systematic examination of something and how to proliferate the idea, through giving it close analysis. Often it's against intuition. For instance you can have three notes, yeah? You can repeat them. And you can have the same three notes rhythmically articulated so it always changes. What's repeated is the gesture. You could make the rhythmic ingredients the same but the notes change. The point is that the accumulation of detail equals the whole.

For you or for the listener?

For both. I want it to be heard. But I don't know if it will and it doesn't matter. That part of the score we've just looked at will make a hell of a noise. I don't know what it'll sound like. But it's not just chaos. I'm not just being expressionist. It's formalised, very rigorous and comes from a fundamental, basic idea which is what we've been talking about.

I'm very concerned about this question in relation to music written today. You know when you pour water into a jar? You know what surface tension is? You can put in too much water, higher than the level of the jar, and it won't spill over, but one drop too much and it does.

It's an issue for Boulez. You pile things up and it cancels out the rest though it may sound spectacular. I go to a lot of trouble to think, how far can I go? How much can I pile in and yet it still retains its individuality?

John Tomlinson said that when he was learning to roar, in the role of the Minotaur, he made a wonderful guttural noise but you said no, it has to be specific, and relate to a word.

That's right. It had to come from a dramatic centre, to have meaning, otherwise it was just a noise and I didn't want that.

OK, that's enough for today?

Yes. I don't want to talk any more. In essence these are the ideas I've been playing around with – as I showed you in those few bars, which may change anyway. It's enough for two lifetimes. I don't need anything else.

6 June 2013

The windows of the Birtwistle house have been thrown open. Old bathroom fittings take up space in front of the house. Harry's son, Silas, is at work making a new bathroom upstairs, banging and whistling. Harry has just returned from nearly three weeks in Japan, where he judged the Siemens Music Prize and heard a concert of his work. Jet lag has sent him into a deep, post-lunch sleep from which he has just woken, surprisingly alert.

In the garden, jackdaws are nesting in the roof. After the intense cold, all has suddenly burst forth. The old plum tree in the middle of the lawn is laden with tiny green beads of fruit like a mass of olives, promising an abundant harvest. The row of quinces, carefully pruned on those cold spring days, are in flower. The older one, with its split branch, seems to have been condemned. 'I'm going to kill it,' Harry says. It's not clear whether he means this intentionally, or inevitably. Tomatoes are on the go in the greenhouse. All are shown, examined, wondered at.

Shall I suggest today's topic?

You'd better. I haven't got a thing in my head. I'm jet-lagged.

You've been away for quite a time – three weeks. Before you left, you had reached a point with the piano concerto where you were getting somewhere, solving interesting problems. You were worried at abandoning it at that point. What happened when you were away? And now you are back, can you pick up where you left off or has everything changed?

I was full of it when I was away. Thinking about it all the time. Because of the problem of jet lag I never seemed to sleep at night, so that meant I kept having thoughts about it . . . And that was hard because I couldn't do anything about it.

And have you gone back to it yet? You've only been home a couple of days . . .

I haven't even dared look at it. The frustration is getting to me. It's like a wound. You've got to take the plaster off. And you know the moment has to be right, otherwise it'll set you back.

There's also something particular about not doing it. The gap between finishing the working day in the evening and starting again the next morning – I'm usually full of ideas in the hours in between, not one of which I ever obey, or use, the next morning. The most potent thing I can do is what comes to me at that time.

Consequently after a longer time – as now, being away – I have even more ideas, and it's even harder.

But I won't even open up the manuscript paper and look at it until I'm in the right condition, mentally, which so far I have not been. I didn't sleep at all last night.

When you were away and thinking of these things . . .

I'll tell you when I think of things: when I'm listening to one of my pieces being performed. I might think, that bit is worth exploring, or why didn't I do that instead . . . ? And that feeds into the next thing I'm working on.

So that's when you do your thinking. Not when you look at Kyoto temples or Japanese gardens?

Oh then too. All the time.

What I'm pleased about was hearing the Violin Concerto in Japan [played by Daniel Hope and the Tokyo Symphony Orchestra, conducted by Stefan Asbury] and the whole question of dialogue. I felt very resolved that I should carry that forward, and that I haven't done enough of that so far.

What have you done so far?

If there is dialogue, it is in longer sentences. The question of dialogue is worth investigating more in this piano concerto. Have we talked about that? We have, haven't we?

Meaning what exactly?

In the traditional idea of a soloist and orchestra, the material is shared. The dialogue takes place using the same material.

And I don't think that's what my Violin Concerto does. It's not an argument either. If there's a dialogue it's between the tutti and the solo violin. The violin never plays its primary material with the orchestra. That is, they don't share it. The orchestra may have secondary material.

We talked about the Beethoven Violin Concerto – I hate making those sorts of comparisons – but very often in it he uses the main material as an accompaniment, as in those opening arpeggios . . . These are things just floating across my mind. We're actually talking about my neurosis. My not being there and doing it . . .

How was it, listening to your Violin Concerto in Tokyo? Your usual frustrations?

There was a realisation, and a frustration. When I was listening to the piece, I was thinking what I'd like to be doing – sitting here and writing the piano concerto – in part prompted by what the piece was suggesting to me.

So your own material – rather than any of the great things you might have encountered as a tourist in Japan – is what has really been stimulating you?

Exactly. In the Japanese temples I was thinking about something else – my piece.

With all these ideas swarming around in your head, do you note them down, just as an aide-memoire?

No. Don't need to. Don't need to. Don't need to.

So it's like a parcel, tied up somewhere in your mind, waiting to be unwrapped . . .

The frustration is I can't do anything about it.

[Silas, whistling, interrupts to say he is going to buy green kitchen scourers. 'You mean you're going to BUY some?' asks Harry, as if Silas had announced he was going to buy a house. 'Is there a particular sort you need?' A short discussion takes place about varieties of kitchen scourer. 'And will you go to the Co-op?' Harry asks, as if there were several other options for their purchase of kitchen basics at 6 p.m. in the sleepy Wiltshire town of Mere.]

And I can't start unlocking those ideas until I'm ready. Maybe I'd make a mistake if I picked the wrong moment . . .

What else did you hear in Tokyo? They performed one concert of your music? How did it go? Was it well received, and well performed?

They did *Exody*. I don't think it's had a good performance. Not one that worked in the way I imagined it would. I was very pleased.

Maybe it's a difficult piece to do. I remember one of your colleagues wrote: 'I just wanted it to stop.' I shouldn't worry. It doesn't make any bloody difference, does it?

In Tokyo I began to remember all the things I put into it. In some ways it was like hearing it for the first time.

There's something about big, famous conductors – they're used to being able to make their orchestras do what they want, and shape the music or the style, because so much of it is so familiar to the players. I'm not criticising them in any way – people like Barenboim or Dohnányi who have done a lot of my music, and have shown a wonderful commitment to it. Barenboim has done *Triumph of Time*, *Exody* and *The Last Supper* . . . all amazing performances.

I think it's to do with different priorities. It's not a question of rehearsing or not. There's never time to do everything. It's priorities. Stefan Asbury, in Japan, seemed to have the same priorities as me, which was about the precision of the music, and it was wonderful to hear. His work-rate, like David Atherton's, is terrific.

Maybe it was the different way a Japanese orchestra is trained, too: very precise, even a little clinical, in a way that can't be moulded in quite the way I'm talking about with, say, the Chicago.

I think that's what it is. They get in front of Wagner and it's all a question of shaping it.

But that's the nature of your music. They may not be used to your idiom. You want precision and clarity. They are accustomed to make things meld.

Yes. It's full of dangers. This piece [*Exody*] is very dense on one level. I suddenly remember what it was I was trying to do. It happened for me. The audience was very enthusiastic.

I remember I wanted to write a piece – I don't know if you've ever tried to put a screw in and tighten it. There's always that little bit more that you can do but you need strength to make that final turn. That's what I wanted to do, to write a piece like that, where you kept turning the material tighter and tighter. And what you do with the screw is you sometimes stop and then have another go, but the screw hasn't – can't – become relaxed.

Anyway it sort of happened for me listening to this performance [of *Exody*]. I don't know if it happened for anyone else and I don't mind really. I'm just talking about how I heard it, and I hadn't heard that before.

They also played a piece called *Imaginary Landscape* for brass, percussion and double basses which I wrote a million years ago. I'd like to rewrite it. I don't like the harmony. I could do it. But I never will. It'll have to be the way it is. He was brilliant with that piece, because it's not easy. It's what you call experimental music. [*Chuckles.*] Very modern. Which is a word – experimental – that I don't like because I think it gives you the right to fail. [*More laughter.*] It's only experimental when it doesn't work. If it works, the experiment has succeeded.

I remember trying to take this up with Berio – who was always rude to me right from the first time I saw him, for some reason.

Why? What sort of rude? Verbally?

That's a good question. No, not verbally. In attitude. I don't know why.

[Silas returns triumphant with scourers.]

HB What did you think, Silas?

SB About what? The scourers?

HB *Exody.*

SB Great title!

HB No no . . .

SB What did I think about that performance in Japan? Or what did I think of that piece?

HB Both.

SB Well, I was very impressed with the conductor, tackling this great monster. And the levels and details and balances, and finding the right voice as it goes through – that all worked. The piece builds and builds, and has an unstoppable momentum.

HB I was saying that. It's the first time . . . You don't know how the next bit is going to be jacked up? Where's the next bit of energy going to come from? From time to time it settles, like a lull in a storm –

SB But also, the woodwind and percussion always work very well but this time the strings were really terrific. And I'd never heard the strings in your music quite like that before.

You'd never really paid much attention to them before, had you?

HB No.

SB The clarity of the rhythms and the way it's put together – it's very complex but you can hear it. I'm not really a musician but you can hear these layers.

FM *[To Silas] Have you heard it much?*

SB No. It hasn't been played too often. I heard it at the Proms and to be honest I didn't remember it much . . . It certainly came across. The early piece [*An Imaginary Landscape*, 1971] was quite good too. I'd never heard it before. You didn't like that much, did you, Dad?

HB Well . . . There's stuff I don't like about it . . .

SB And there are two tubas in *Exody* – big boy stuff. But then *Gawain* has . . .

HB Three. Three tubas – tubae – in *Gawain*.

SB So how many did Wagner have?

HB That's different. That was more about doubling – you can have as many to a part as you want. Like he had all those harps . . .

SB   Really?

HB   Yes, and they're all playing Steve Reich really, what?
     They're all pedalling the same chord . . .

[Silas goes off with his scourers to continue work upstairs
in the bathroom.]

*Can we make a big switch and talk about your fascination with
early music, especially English Tudor music, for example?*

There are influences you borrow, consciously, and there are
influences which come in under the floor with the draught,
which you have no control over.
     People have always said I'm an 'English Composer'. And
as it's the one thing I self-consciously always tried to avoid,
I'm never quite sure what it is. Have you seen that book by
Pevsner about the Englishness of English art? It's very
interesting, that. He's asking the same question. What is
particularly English?
     And Arkane [Nakanishi], my Japanese student, she's accused
of being an English composer . . . because she studied with me.

What do you think that means?

I don't know. I think there's a certain European avant-garde,
certain elements, that don't apply to me . . .

Shall we go back to early music?

I've told you about history of music at Manchester? In year one, in order to give you a historical grounding in music, they did a weekly thing on a Monday morning, ten o'clock, going through aspects of classical music. It began with Bach. Time itself began with Bach! I think modernism was dealt with in a week. That was how I first remember encountering Sandy – a voice from the back of the hall, articulate, distinctive, wonderfully clear, taking issue with the lecturer. That was Sandy! He was in touch with the radical side of music and had a degree of intellectual sophistication which was new to me.

Anyway, I remember trying to express the fact that there must have been two thousand years before that and they said yes, that was called 'Pre-Bach'!

Did anyone teach that?

No, they just ignored it. Pre-Bach! The Dark Ages. A place where you didn't go. So of course no one was performing it.

Not even Byrd or Tallis?

Not that I knew of. I think to be honest it was Max, studying at the University, who really got me going. Together we became a pair of medievalists. Max was always very keen on angels. [*Chuckles.*]

But there was one particular piece, published by L'Oiseau-Lyre, called *Hoquetus David* by Machaut [1300–1377]. It's the great enigmatic piece. I made a version when I was in the Army for the band to play.

You had that published?

No. I did another later. This was probably for wind band. Then I wrote a piece called *Machaut à ma manière* and that's an arrangement of it. I did one for the Pierrot Players. On an aeroplane to Italy.

But the Machaut is an enigma. I'm sure musicologists could tell me why it is the way it is. But I could never work out what the decisions were, for its continuity. You know, what was the process of getting from one note to another? The way it's expressed – I've never seen the original – there's no suggestion of tempo anywhere. I've heard a dreadful performance, you couldn't believe how awful it was . . .

Fast? Slow?

Very slow. I made it very fast. That aspect of it becomes very intriguing – stylistically why Palestrina, for instance, has defining ingredients, as does Lassus or Victoria or Byrd. You can think of music like a recipe. What goes into your cake? What makes it one cake instead of another? What makes the same ingredients different when someone else bakes it?

In other works, what is the essence that makes something like it is? What are the decisions? That period of music is unlike any other. Bach's a bit of a problem – not a problem but that same question of how he got to the next bit. Whereas when you get to Haydn and Mozart you can hear what the journey is, what the moment is. You think, ah, he's done that. Or he's contrasted this with this. It's not easy but at least you can get hold of it.

Why did it interest you?

There's a sort of fascination. I had that same interest for years in the music of Dunstable. I never heard a note. But I knew it from *Musica Britannica*. No one ever performed it except in arrangements I made for fellow students – the clarinet class and that. I did it in the Army. It wasn't till a long time later I organised some concerts and suggested doing some Dunstable. It was a terrible disappointment!

Really? Why?

Because of the way they sang it. The rhythmical aspect was all rounded off. It wasn't how I thought of it at all. Or how I performed it with my clarinet classes. But that was about performance, not the music itself. So disappointing. It had become sort of neutralised. I wanted something raw and rhythmically articulated. Maybe they sing it too slowly.

But Machaut is the one who always seems to be on your horizon.

Because of the Hocket. It's in three parts. And then there's the quint, which doubles the parts a fifth higher on the organ, which is why it's called quint.

Did you use that device?

An imitation of it. I made my own version so it would sound as I wanted.

There was a sort of pivotal moment when I went with Sandy to the Royal Academy and there was an exhibition of Picasso's *Las Meninas*. You know those works? He did his own version of Velázquez. And so I did a piece for the Sinfonietta, one of those impossible Flemish pieces with the rhythmical complexities taken ad nauseam. I can't remember what the technique is called . . . *ars subtilior*? It's a collection from a particular school where rhythm is impossibly complex. In singing you can round it off, but with instruments it remains angular. What I intend to do is, whatever the journey is from the orginal, I intend to take it a step further. I'm going to make an arrangement of my arrangement, for the same forces. So they can play one next to the other.

Together?

No. One, then the other!

I've done Bach too, organ preludes. I did that when I was at Canary Wharf. I did it for a ballet – *Bach Measures*. It's arrangements of the *Little Organ Book*. I suppose it's an act of love, like owning them. It was going to that Picasso with Sandy that started me, or gave me the courage. Max did a lot of arrangements too . . .

Do you think painters find it easier, or more accepted to do this? In music it's called an arrangement, with an implied criticism.

It's what you leave. It makes it more like itself.

They [the London Sinfonietta] are doing a recording next year of some of my pieces and I want to put this to them as an idea. Maybe they should start with the original and then gradually it moves through an arrangement. Or I might go the opposite way, back into the original piece. We'll see.

Have a look at my arrangements. I added some things. But the Bach are fantastic pieces, absolutely wonderful and they're sort of wasted on the organ as they're never heard. They're all chorale preludes . . . Anyway it was danced at the Queen Elizabeth Hall.

[Silas reappears, having finished scouring, and takes over the conversation. Harry leaves the room.]

SB   I was compiling a list of opposites about Dad though I don't know where it was taking me.

Go on.

SB   You've got the land of the living and the underworld in *The Second Mrs Kong*, well in all of them really. So there's that vertical thing. Then there's the more horizontal one in *Gawain* – the inside and the outside. The Green Knight knocks at the door and comes into the court. And then there are these worlds that co-exist. In *Gawain* again, you've got a theatrical world, of the pantomime horse. It wouldn't work with a real one. Then in *Down by the Greenwood Side* you've got the world of the Mummers' play and Mrs Green.

You said something earlier about English landscape?

SB I've noticed he gets asked is his music 'English' and he shrugs his shoulders and says he doesn't know. But there's all that stuff during the war and after – that's what he knew. Playing in the military band and panto-mime. Then there was a reaction against it with Max and Sandy and not wanting to seem sentimental and pastoral, but fiery Manchester boys, against all of that.

He always says the landscapes are strictly musical. But he's never admitted, or no one's ever probed him enough, to bring out those feelings for where we grew up on Raasay, and France – he loved it. These musical landscapes do have a personal, poetic side to them.

How much more 'ancient-English' could, say, Silbury Air *be?*

SB Exactly. Or those flute duets, *Duets for Storab*. People would say to him, 'This landscape must inspire you', and he'd say no, I could work in a dungeon, but I don't know whether that's strictly true. Or I'd be interested to hear him talk more about that. I've talked to him about when he was a kid. He moved from the centre of Oswaldtwistle where his mum and dad had a baker's shop to the countryside – or that's what you could see from the window, Childers Green.

I knew it too, because my grandfather continued to live there. Down the lane there was a bit of woodland surrounded by cliffs, Dad said he knew it well. He was an only child and spent a lot of time in that place. It reminded me of Auden in his limestone quarry and his invented world. I think that was an experience, the wildlife, I think it was a revelation . . . It's probably going from one extreme to another, at that particular age.

There used to be big cooling towers, almost in the back garden.

When Tom [Phillips] did the portrait of Harry in 1995 for the National Portrait Gallery, Harry asked him to include those cooling towers.

SB They've gone now.

Did you know what he was doing, or working on, when you were a child?

SB I was certainly aware. I mean he got up and went to work down the garden. I think it was Adam who, when asked to fill in a form saying 'Father's place of work', wrote 'End of the garden'.

Could you interrupt him?

SB Oh, I did, yes. It wasn't a problem. It wasn't forbidden territory. In Twickenham he had this plywood shed that had a Perspex dome on the top. There was a plum tree growing over it and all you could hear were the branches squeaking. He's told you about all his work places – the octagons, etc.? The one on Raasay was made of breeze-blocks and covered in pebbledash. It was a sort of chapter house. The one in France was beautiful. It had thick walls, and dressed stone with a Quercy roof – particular to the

[SB] part of France where Mum and Dad lived in the Lot. They have quite a steep pitch and then splay out at the bottom. It must have cost a fortune. It took ages. As far as I know he wrote *Gawain* and then he left. It seemed like that.

I remember as a kid going to hear the Sinfonietta at the Queen Elizabeth Hall and there'd be a little crowd of us in the front row and the rest was empty.

What did you think?

SB Well, sometimes there were people there! But going to *The Minotaur* at Covent Garden the other day, it was packed . . . I'm just aware of that comparison.

I don't remember a lot of concerts really. I think I always felt, and still do, although he often says, 'I don't know what I'm doing' or 'This is rubbish', that there's always this sense of confidence. You felt he always knew what was going on, what he was doing. He wasn't down there pulling his hair out. He was always quite calm. It's a slow process, spending several days writing a couple of seconds of music. Amazing really, isn't it?

I think it's always going on as well, in his head. I remember once, in the very early days, going back to his dad, there was one of these BBC recorded studio events. It was a little invited audience, maybe thirty people. Dad was conducting. I can't remember what it was. I remember sitting next to Mum and Grandad and there was a pregnant pause in the middle. And Grandad, who was a bit deaf, turned to Mum and said in a voice that everyone could hear, 'Is our 'Arry done yet?'

But he was proud?

SB   Oh yeah . . . definitely.

You said the compositional process is always going on. Can you tell? Or, how can you tell?

SB   Yes, you can. He gestures. If you're going for a walk or something you can see these gestures . . . I don't know what they are. He's always done them. Waving his arm in a particular way. Maybe it's something completely different.

Did he bring his work problems back into the house? Was he temperamental, or phlegmatic?

SB   No, he'd come in and cook instead. He was always very jolly. He used to, as he still does, walk down the garden and examine his little plants.

We just looked at the enormous crop of plums on their way . . .

SB   I guess it must have been pretty hard, having three children and all the rest, and no proper 'job' until he went to the National. Mum really did all the family stuff and was always there and part of the equation. Great cook. Quite eccentric in her own quiet way. She used to be a singer, but she gave it up. She had all these little obsessions to do with health foods, and little ointments for this or that.

Was there an expectation that you would be interested in music?

SB Well, I still try. I play classical guitar – I love it, it's good fun. He's just written a piece for guitar. I can't get beyond the first bar . . .

[Harry returns.]

HB Everything all right? What do you think of the [bathroom] tiles? They're very matt, aren't they? Do you know how to make . . . ?

SB Hot chocolate? Whisky sour?

HB No. *Vongole* . . . is that what they're called? *Spaghetti vongole.*

SB Have you got some? In their shells? Where did you get those? Waitrose?

HB No, the fishmonger in Shaftesbury.

[The conversation moves on to garlic, tomatoes, oil, sweating onions, Italian recipes . . .]

*

Harry has instilled his passion for cooking into each of his sons. Whereas Silas and Toby were around on more than one occasion during our conversations, his artist son Adam was at home in France. Originally I planned to include here only the extract below from an interview Adam and I carried out in 2012 for his exhibition at Kings Place, London (which opened with a concert of Harry's music, a first public collaboration between father and son), but later we supplemented it with a telephone conversation.

From Kings Place magazine (Spring, 2012) interview:

AB As a child I always wanted to draw and paint. My father encouraged me. We are close but he's quite elusive. Although he is a composer there wasn't any music round the house except a tiny radio in the kitchen. I remember buying a record player when I was about fourteen and annoying my father by playing pop music when he was trying to work . . . My mother didn't say much one way or the other about my art but they both let me do what I wanted, were always behind me and never obstructed me. Even when I failed all of my 'O' and 'A' levels I still managed to get into art school – you could in those days, around 1980, if you showed you really wanted to do it. At Chelsea I mainly did sculpture and then thought, what do I do now? By then my parents were living in France so I went there and began painting Harry. I was lucky that a lot of their friends who came to stay were people I could paint, so I began to earn a living: Pierre Boulez, Alfred Brendel, Morton Feldman, Hans Werner Henze. That's where it all really started.

From a later telephone conversation:

[143]

Can you say more about having a composer – specifically Harry! – as your dad?

AB   I got quite complacent about it. He was just doing what he did: writing music. I wasn't aware that he'd ever had another job – like selling ironing boards, before I was born. As a young child I remember him going off every morning at 7 a.m. to teach. Then he won a Harkness Scholarship and we all went off to America on a huge liner, the *SS France*, which took about five days. I think he was writing *Punch and Judy* at Princeton, though I had no concept of what that meant exactly. I was about six. After a year we moved to Colorado.

I remember in another house we stayed in, in Swarthmore, Pennsylvania, he had a room upstairs with a desk in it and he'd disappear in there. There was a big black maid in a uniform – this was the early 1960s – and she was clearly puzzled by why he would go into a room without a bed for two hours or so, which she wasn't allowed to go in and clean, then come out and wander round, exactly as he still does and, as it happens, as I do when I'm working.

And one day her curiosity got the better of her and she said, 'Massa Harry – what you doin' in there? Whatever you doin', Massa Harry, you sure am a quiet man'!

He worked – as he still does – with these big drawing boards. I was already pretty busy with my drawing and painting and making mobiles . . . and I went in and drew all over his desk. I do remember him coming in and saying, 'Who's drawn all over this desk?' and I said,

'Not me not me not me.' Of course it was obvious it was me.

Both Toby and Silas ended up attending several schools. Was that true for you too?

AB   Yes, I was often left pretty much to my own devices. I went, all told, to eighteen different schools. I think the early bit was OK but by secondary level I was left to my own devices. At one time when we were in America – Pennsylvania – I hated it so much that after nine months I went to live with Peter Zinovieff and his family in Putney. Then I didn't go to school for ages, when I was about fourteen – maybe a month or two. I was sent to a crammer to be crammed with information, but that didn't work. For a while I went to a fourth-rate boarding school in Berkshire which had an inspirational art master – David Kirchner, nephew of the great German Expressionist Ernst Ludwig Kirchner – but after one year and two weeks I was expelled for smoking dope. The headmaster said, 'This is Police Detective so-and-so from the drugs corp. Do you realise you can be put to death for this crime?'

   Anyway, I got on the train and went home to Twickenham. Dad was working at the National Theatre at the time. When I walked in he said, 'What are you doing here?' I explained and he said, 'Fuck 'em!'

He and your mother weren't cross?

AB   No, I don't think so. They just thought it was all silly . . .

Can you see similarities in the way you and Harry work?

AB   Apart from the working then wandering around, no,
we're quite different. His approach is a balance of
intellect and spontaneity. He wants to work out what
notes he's putting down and whether what he hears in
his head will be what he hears when musicians play the
score. I can be far more spontaneous and instinctive: I
make a mark and the painting is under way.

I've painted or drawn him about thirty times – there's
one on public view at the Royal Academy of Music and
another in the National Portrait Gallery. I think early
on, when I was living with them in France, he volun-
teered himself as a subject because he thought I should
try drawing from life. We don't really discuss work and
are more likely to share time fishing or cooking.

All my paintings of him are called *Birtwistle by
Birtwistle* except the most recent, which shows him in
front of a piece of meat and is called *Cow Chop*. In fact
Silas and I are here in France now, about to cook a pig
leg – complete with crackling which French butchers
don't usually sell – which will be ready in about five
hours . . . Dad's probably more likely to follow a recipe,
at least initially, than I am. I tend to look at the picture
then make it up.

*Has he spoken much of his awareness of his dyslexia, which he
sees as a key part of who he is?*

AB I'm the same as him. I look at a page and start reading three paragraphs down instead of at the top . . . And I'm not too good in the spelling department, but it doesn't matter so much today with spellchecks and so on as it would have done for him.

Have you talked much about his childhood?

AB Yes, quite a bit. You know about his parents having a bakery? There are plenty of stories . . . Has he told you that he used to be given the same Christmas present each year – I don't know how long this went on; maybe it only happened once – he was given a train set then halfway through the year he had it taken away then got given it again at Christmas! Then there was his best friend Peter Lee.

The one who was good at everything, including playing the piano?

AB Yes. One year Peter got given a brand-new bicycle. And Dad was given his old one . . . !

That's too sad. Did he talk about school?

AB There's one thing he told me. That, probably in secondary school, he decided to make the school disappear because he hated it so much. He knew the only way he could do it was by a method no one would notice. So he and some of his chums took a brick away each day.

[AB] I don't know how long for or how far they got . . . you'll
have to ask him.

Harry remembers things slightly differently, though is happy
to let Adam tell the stories as they exist in his mind. This is
part of a telephone conversation after the book has been
submitted, when I ring to check a few facts.

What happened about the toys?

That still saddens me. Because my parents worked at the
weekend, I was always sent off to an aunt. I had a set of toys
there. Little figures made of lead: soldiers, animals, that sort
of thing. I knew every one of these figures like the back of
my hand. Exactly how they felt and where the paint was
chipped. One Christmas, they were wrapped up and I was
given them as my present on Christmas morning. I still recall
that disappointment.

And what about Peter Lee and the bike?

Ah, that's something else. Not at all the same sort of thing. I
totally stripped that bike down, replaced the tyres and brakes,
cleaned it, painted it – and made it completely my own. I
only have to think of that bike and I can smell 3-in-One.
You know what that is? OK. Or the other way round – I just
have to smell 3-in-One and I'm on that bike, away and free.

12–14 June 2013

No conversations take place during this period. Harry is in Aldeburgh for the premiere of *Songs from the Same Earth*. At a pre-concert talk – standing room only – David Harsent reads the poems and says Harry doesn't intervene or change lines but sometimes asks for more. In *The Minotaur*, when Ariadne realises she is to be abandoned, Harry needed words to express her emotion, which resulted in the Lament, one of the key moments in the opera.

He and David Harsent remember differently how the title of the song cycle came about. Did Harry make it up after David had completed the poems? No, Harry says, they were called *From the Same Earth*, 'and I said can you call it *Songs from the Same Earth*?' That is the nature of their collaboration.

Mark Padmore and the pianist Andrew West give a successful premiere on a chilly, bright evening at Snape Maltings.

Later, at dinner in the Red House – once the home of Britten and Pears, whose wraiths still seem to rest in the skirting – Harsent says he tried two other settings but they didn't work for Harry. 'I said, "Why not, Harry?" And he said, "I can't set the word 'underpass'." And I said, "Don't be silly, Harry. You can set any word. Could you set the word 'Fuck'?" After a long pause Harry said, "No." Whatever the reason he didn't want to set these texts, but it didn't matter because I'd written them, they exist as poems and they gave me fresh material for my latest collection [*Night* (Faber)]!'

After the concert, performers and friends gather at a supper in the Red House. Tom Phillips, whose several drawings and paintings of Harry include one that hangs at home in Mere, interrupts proceedings to present a drawing of his design for the Britten centenary fifty-pence piece, soon to be issued by the Royal Mint. From his pocket he retrieves a prototype, one of only two yet in existence, which is passed around. 'Artists like to make editions,' he observes. 'This will be an edition of eighteen million. But no royalties, alas.' Britten is the first composer to appear on a UK coin. Harry says, as an aside later, that he was instrumental in getting Elgar on the twenty-pound note (out of circulation since 2010). 'You were "instrumental", Harry?' I ask. 'Or maybe I should say I "orchestrated" it . . .' the composer replies.

Next morning, Harry is to be found eating scrambled eggs in a café on Aldeburgh High Street where the cast of *Peter Grimes*, preparing for the Britten 100 performance on the beach, have congregated all week. Harry and David Harsent are collaborating again. He has just had confirmation of a new commission from the Royal Opera House's Linbury Theatre for a companion piece to *The Corridor*, the theatre work for two voices which was premiered at Aldeburgh in 2009. Mark Padmore was the tenor.

An hour later, Padmore himself wanders down Aldeburgh High Street with a bag of shopping. Yes, he was pleased with the premiere of *Songs from the Same Earth*. He doesn't say much but looks at once joyful and relieved. Had the piece been hard? 'Early on it was quite hard . . . It's hard when you first receive a new work from a composer, and you want to say thank you, it's wonderful. But you don't know what it is until you start working on it, and finding out what the music is. Only then can you give a proper response. These are truly wonderful songs.'

Later, on the phone, David Harsent and I spoke further.

How did you meet Harry?

DH I wrote a book-long poem sequence called *Mister Punch*. In reviewing it for the *Observer*, Peter Porter drew parallels between my collection and Harry's opera, *Punch and Judy*. Harry saw the review, got the book (or so I imagine) and (obviously) found things to like in it. He called me: a cold call, as it were. We'd never met. When he said, 'It's Harry Birtwistle,' it took me a moment or two to work out who it was. He said, 'I thought you might like to write an opera with me.' Of course, he had a subject in mind: composers almost always do. When he told me he wanted a version of *Sir Gawain and the Green Knight*, I was sold on the idea immediately: it's a benchmark for any English poet.

I'd seen *Punch and Judy* at the Drill Hall, so I assumed *Gawain* would be on at a similar sort of venue. Harry and I had been talking about the piece for some time before he happened to mention it would be main stage at the Royal Opera House. We had a few meetings. It was quickly apparent that we would be able to work together.

How does the relationship between writer and composer work for you and Harry?

DH We've collaborated, now, on five pieces – a sixth is in progress – and it's always been a very rewarding experience. We talk a lot about the piece before I start to write, but once we're agreed on a way forward, I go away and write the libretto. I might call him a couple of times during that process to let him know about a change of direction or some new thought if the thought in question alters things, but largely speaking I produce the libretto in isolation. When it's done (and after I've put the piece through three or four drafts of my own) there might be a few minor revisions, but Harry has never asked me to cut a line, or taken exception to some passage or another.

Once he starts to compose – then the changes occur. The weight of his composition starts to tell on mine, which is as it should be. But it's always a matter of more text, not of cuts. On one occasion he called asking for more lines for Ariadne [in the *Minotaur*] in order to round out a scene and help the audience know more about the character. His theatrical instinct is very strong: he really understands theatre and how it works. 'Just a little aria,' he said. 'Oh, and make it dark.' I pointed out that 'dark' is my default mode. 'I know,' he said, 'but go darker.' The upshot was some lines beginning, 'The Cretan sun is black . . .' When Christine Rice sang the lines in rehearsal it was electrifying. Tony Pappano was standing near by. He said, 'That's you and Harry at your best.' The odd – but perhaps significant – thing is that the moment came because Harry asked for it: it was an add-on.

Did Gawain *go smoothly? What was Harry's first reaction to your text?*

DH My wife and I were on holiday in France just after I'd finished the libretto for *Gawain*. We took a diversion to the back of beyond, where Harry was living, to deliver the text. It was mid-afternoon. Harry's wife, Sheila, answered the door and said, 'He's in the kiosk.' Harry took the same basic plans of his garden studio with him whenever he moved house and had it rebuilt: an octagonal structure; the French didn't know what to call it, so it became '*le kiosk*'. I knocked on the door. Harry emerged, blinking, into the sunlight of Lot-et-Garonne. I handed over my libretto. He weighed it in his hand, as if it were on a scale, and said, 'It's not fucking *Siegfried*, is it?' – meaning, I assumed, it might be a bit short for a full-length, main-stage opera. I said, 'It'll play long, Harry.' And it did – so long that, for the revival at Covent Garden, we had to lose the twenty-two-minute masque from the end of Act 1, because the orchestra was into overtime. There's a concert performance of *Gawain* at the Barbican next year. Harry and I have just taken a chunk out of Act 2. After the Salzburg Festival performance (which neither of us liked) we decided the second act had some longueurs. We'll see how it plays . . .

I think it's true to say that Harry and I have become close in the twenty-five years that we've been working together. He has an acute and very interesting mind. We've never argued or fallen out. We're both interested

[DH] in places of darkness, in netherworlds, in the people who dare to go to such places. I said, once, that if Harry and I each dreamed about the piece we were working on, it would be a different version of the same dream.

23 June 2013

WILTSHIRE. SUMMER SOLSTICE. COLD, BLUSTERY, RAINY. TEMPERATURE 14 DEGREES.

Tall evening primroses, white peonies and roses look forlorn in the wind. Harry stands in his studio with big pieces of manuscript paper spread around not one but two walls. 'I've got in a muddle – I don't know what order they're in. Maybe it doesn't matter.' Today's tea, a deep orange, roasted variety, is one of several brought back from Japan.

Another acquisition in Japan is a sharp chopping knife made, he explains, in the same way as samurai swords: stainless steel either side with a soft metal in the middle. A Japanese inscription is engraved on one side of the lethal blade. On the other it says 'HARLSSON [*sic*] BIRTWISTLE'. Did he need a kitchen knife with his name on? It could set a false trail if ever found at a murder scene. 'If I'd had the wit to think of it when they asked I'd have said, "No thank you",' he replies, chopping a heap of parsley – at lightning speed – for an omelette.

You've had a lot of interruptions – Japan, Aldeburgh, people filming you for Salzburg . . .

That filming was terrible. They kept asking me to walk down the garden . . . Could I just do it again? And again. I said, could I put my coat on because it was cold and they said that would spoil the continuity because I'd be there with my coat on and without it on. How daft is that? What continuity?

How are you getting back to working on the piano concerto? Have you managed to? Are the ideas that were bubbling at the time of your departure for Tokyo still there?

I addressed the possible continuity on a piece of paper – what I thought it was going to be.

In notes? In words?

In words, very simply. Because the idea in front of you is not clear, you can't articulate it fully. I can never say precisely what I'm heading towards. When you say words, they're not words that would mean much, or relate specifically to the idea. One of the phrases was 'get thin' and it wasn't talking about me. I wrote the words on the page. I left off, before going to Salzburg, at a tutti. I wrote it there. It's not addressed to anyone. I know what it means.

But it won't stay in the score?

No. And I didn't get thin! But now, several pages on, I'm getting thin . . . Try to understand that I thought I'd got to a point in the piece where there was going to be a move. When I came back I prolonged the thing of slimming it down. I composed two or three pages of music and it's getting thin in a way I never imagined. Does that make any sense?

In fact I would never imagine I'd be writing what I've just written at all. And now I'm gonna get thin . . . but it's a different thinness.

I'm always reminded of Morty [Feldman]. He was the first composer that I found – not so much in the music he wrote but in the way he thought about it – I could talk to. We were very close. It seems to me that one of my problems about music is that it's always technical.

Do you mean your own problems are technical? Or what?

I mean that when you read or talk about music, it's always about technical questions. But I've certainly got more in thinking about the process itself from painters, rather than composers. Painting deals with the process directly. Morton Feldman's way of thinking was very much influenced by the American painters.

Rothko?

Any of them. Rothko. Guston. There's a conversation with Guston in this book . . .

[Philip Guston: *Collected Writings, Lectures and Conversations* (University of California Press, 2010) is on the table.]

Morty and I talked a lot about music and one of his favourite words was 'moves'. He used to say he liked my moves! His moves were not quite so obvious. But when you start thinking about moves – listen to Beethoven. I've said this before. He never does what you think he's going to and yet it's logical and illogical. It's not there just for the sake of effect.

If you want to find the moves in Morty's music you'd be hard pushed. Do you know his music? It's true minimalism. It comes back to what we were talking about: when I leave off a piece I think I know where I'm going, as in when you look at the road ahead in the car headlights. But in fact I don't know what I'm going to do tomorrow morning. No idea. At any point you can go anywhere. It depends where my intuition leads me.

Looking later at the Guston book I find this from Feldman, in response to a question on how he learned music:

MF I don't know how I learned. I learned through a kind of osmosis, I think. I think I learned more trying to avoid learning anything. I think I learned, more than anybody else, just trying to avoid learning. It's a lot of work trying to avoid learning. But that's a problem. My students know more than I do [. . .] Oh, they know more about music history. They know more acoustical phenomena. They can tell you exactly how a violin is constructed [. . .] They could be like guys that mix their own paints, instead of buying it from a tube. If I learned anything, the most important thing I ever learned from other music was to admire something that is totally unlike myself. But then I can't learn anything *from* it. I always had that paradox in my life with Varèse. I mean

[MF] no one could be so totally different, and yet I'm just nuts about Varèse, and I can't figure out why I should be so nuts about Varèse. [Guston, p. 92]

Feldman also talks about periods of history during which everyone thought the old systems were dying out (a view Harry has also expressed).

MF The end of the nineteenth century was very much like that, after Wagner took tonality as far as anybody else really took tonality. And for about forty years they didn't know what to do with this new chromatic harmony because it wasn't really systematised. Then Schoenberg came along and systematised a much more complicated scale [. . .] But the great guy was a guy that made moves in this ambivalence between periods. Webern, before he got influenced by Schoenberg, in 1906 wrote a piece called *Six Pieces for Orchestra* which is absolutely phenomenal. Listen to this piece. Get it, as painters get it. You never heard such colour in your life. Really, he was looking ahead, he was looking backwards, but still he moved. He still moved. And it's fantastic. [Guston, p. 93]

How did you come to know Feldman?

Through my then publisher, Bill Colleran. And I went to Buffalo, New York, where he was a professor of composition.

Toby Birtwistle, Harry's youngest son, has vivid memories of that time in Buffalo:

TB I was nine years old when I met Morton Feldman, when we were living in Buffalo. We paid several visits to his apartment. He was very keen that I was well catered for and not bored while the others talked and so set me up at his very tall desk with paper and coloured pencils. A very chatty man with a strong New York accent which I loved as I was honing it myself having to swear allegiance to the flag every morning, he was also keen on a recent advert for a drink that sold grapefruit soda pop featuring a polar bear. So Morton would shout across the kitchen to me, 'Hey Toby! Wanna soda? "It's reeeeaallll FROTHY, MAN!!"' That was the tagline. He was interactive and friendly and always reminded me of Benny Hill when he was playing that Chinese feller. You should ask Dad about the story of the time he and Morton met the hobo in New York City . . . Very funny.

So, Harry, would you say he was a big influence? Like Boulez? Like Max and Sandy? And if different, in what ways?

Different ingredients completely. One thing that Boulez did for me, in my insecurity as a composer, and where I felt I came from, I think he – without saying a word – was a terrific encouragement. I can't say that in my make-up or my journey as a composer I knew what I was doing. They both, Boulez and Feldman, encouraged me. Not only the kind of music Boulez wrote but the fact that he played mine – the two elements are linked. I think I'm talking about rites of passage. That's what both of them were for me, in their way. Without saying anything, they helped me write my music.

But in neither case was it anything to do with writing like them. Though I think *Le Marteau sans maître* is the kind of piece, in all the noise of contemporary music that's gone on in my lifetime, I'd like to have written. It's a very important piece. Carter's Double Concerto is very interesting too, though I wouldn't immediately include Carter in the same group of influences.

For a piece of light entertainment, tell me some of the other pieces you'd like to have written. It's a phrase you've used before.

Light entertainment? Oh yes, that's me all over.

Well, you can't talk about Schubert, can you? I'd like to have written some of that. But if I make a list I become a kind of music lover . . . Or maybe in the end that's what it's all about.

I do wonder why composers I talk to don't like Rachmaninov but do like Mussorgsky.

You agree, disagree?

Oh, I agree, I love Mussorgsky. You know I can't stand Rachmaninov. It's the same with Prokofiev and Stravinsky. I don't like Prokofiev. Why one and not the other? Why Stravinsky, why Mussorgsky? Scriabin nearly gets there.

Do you know the game they used to play in Princeton? It's called horse, bird, muffin. It was discussed over coffee, and a constant source of fun and interest. You simply put things in those three categories and you can't have subcategories. They're all equal. The muffin isn't worse than the horse, even though it sounds it.

Top Harrison Birtwistle *c.*1947 – 'I was probably about thirteen' – playing clarinet. He is in the uniform of the North East Lancashire Military Band.

Bottom The North East Lancashire Military Band *c.*1948, with Harrison Birtwistle second from left in second row. He appears to be the youngest player by at least a decade.

Top left Harry, upright in the middle, during National Service at Oswestry, Shropshire.

Top right A melancholy snap from his clean-shaven army days, aged twenty-one.

Bottom The 'Manchester Group' as students *c.*1955. Clockwise from top left: Harry, John Ogdon, Elgar Howarth, Peter Maxwell Davies, John Dow, Audrey Goehr and Alexander Goehr. Harry's shirt once belonged to George Formby, 'who gave it to a drunken publican who gave it to my father'.

Top Portrait of the composer as a young man, in characteristic pose with manuscript paper, *c.*1960.

Bottom left At Cranborne Chase, where Harry taught in the 1960s. 'It was the era of the Beatles. I'm wearing a Beatle jacket.'

Bottom right 'The three musketeers': Silas, Toby and Adam Birtwistle in the mid-1960s.

Top With Elizabeth Wilson, cellist, writer and one-time pupil of Harry's at Cranborne Chase, and her then husband, the pianist Radu Lupu.

Centre left Sharing a joke over dinner with Michael Tippett at a festival in their joint honour, Rotterdam, May 1988.

Centre right With Melinda Maxwell at the Purcell Room, mid-1980s, rehearsing *Pulse Sampler* (1981) for oboe and claves, one of several works Harry has written for her. (© Richard Hubert Smith)

Bottom With Pierre Boulez, deep in conversation at the Royal Festival Hall.

Top Rehearsing *Bow Down* at the National Theatre, with the poet Tony Harrison playing a bamboo flute.

Bottom On the set of *The Second Mrs Kong*, Glyndebourne, 1994.

Top left 'Ah, definitely in Raasay,' says Harry. 'No, definitely in Lunegarde,' says his son, Adam. 'OK, it must be France,' Harry concedes.

Top right Preparing *confit d'oie* in France, mid-1980s. Harry has always taken his cooking seriously.

Bottom Harry and his wife Sheila at home in France, mid-1980s.

Top Cowchop 2012 by Adam Birtwistle. Of the many he has completed, this is the artist's favourite painting of his father.

Bottom Drawing on pastel by Tom Phillips RA (1995), one of a series in preparation for an oil-on-canvas portrait owned by the National Portrait Gallery.

Top At the kitchen table in Mere, 2013, with Afghan bowls of lemons and quinces and, behind, the blue drawers from Uncle Edgar.

Bottom Harrison Birtwistle walking on Whitesheet Hill, Wiltshire, summer 2013.

OK, go on.

Right, Beethoven, Mozart, Brahms. It's quite obvious really.

The horse is the difficult one?

No, Beethoven is the horse. So Mozart's the bird and Brahms is the muffin.
   Berg, Schoenberg and Webern?
   Boulez, Stockhausen, Ligeti?

So Ligeti is the bird . . . ? Can you have two horses?

Na na na na. That's not the game. I think Stockhausen is the muffin and Boulez is the horse.

What are you?

I'm not prepared to say.

You're the horse?

You think I'm a horse?

Well, maybe a bit of bird and a bit of muffin.

You can't do that. That's why the game's interesting.
   Can you imagine a piece of music that you know? That you know very well?

OK. Brahms's Fourth Symphony.

And what do you hear?

The opening, bits of different movements.

But don't you get a sense of the whole thing? It's as if the whole piece is sounding in your head. It's got nothing to do with the particular details. It's as if the entire piece is there, as if time is in a ball. And that's a bit how it is before I write a piece. It's as if the whole piece is there. I know what it is before I've even written it, but in other ways I don't know at all. As I unravel it, it never turns out to be what you think it's going to be. Then there's the question of the context – of unravelling one's intuition without the cliché.

The key question is how do you avoid cliché? How can you compose the journey?

Now I wouldn't want this to get misunderstood. It's not a question of always trying to be novel.

This is hard. I'm very clear about this in my head. I've said before about this idea of being in a permanent state of exposition, or discontinuity.

Music exists in time. It's to do with your memory. You hear everything in retrospect in a way, whatever it is. What I'm trying to do is illuminate the immediate past. When we talk about time, are we talking about one note, ten notes? What can the memory hold?

What I'm talking about is how you compose the next element to illuminate what you've just heard – the immediate past. I'm not interested in just doing things for the sake of it, or doing things for the sake of doing it differently. The interesting question is how time moves. It comes back to Morton Feldman and the question of 'moves' . . .

Where I am now, and when I thought I knew where I was going – well, I know I won't actually go to either tomorrow morning. I can't just write something and fill out an idea, as if music is a piece of architecture or the plot to a crime novel. I have to believe in the moment. It's a sort of spontaneity except there's no such thing as spontaneity, the big brush in composition. The big brush would take me a couple of days, at least.

What about the Messiaen idea you mentioned – the Oiseaux exotiques *reference as a way of finishing the concerto?*

I've abandoned that. I stopped thinking about it. I was reacting to a context. Now I can see it won't work. It might come back to me but you won't recognise it.

I think all this time we've been talking, we're clarifying the same issues – including starting off with John Wayne, all those weeks ago.

8 July 2013

CLOUDLESS SKY. BREATHLESS, STILL DAY. EXTREMELY HOT. AVERAGE TEMPERATURE 29 DEGREES.

Harry is finishing a session with a composer he guides – he prefers not to say 'teaches' – Lynne Plowman. 'She has a job and a child and she composes too. And she's making fast progress.' In the kitchen plans are afoot for a Tuscan bean salad. I note the ingredients: white beans (cannellini), half onion thinly sliced and rinsed in water, 5 × good anchovies, cucumber, tomato, lemon, oil, salt. 'I eat a lot of beans,' he notes, without consequence.

Harry is wearing a karate-style cross-over tied loose jacket and loose trousers. Purchased in Japan? 'Oh I affected the Japanese style before that . . . Good for hot weather.' With barely a pause for niceties he starts talking.

Something happened this morning. I walked down the garden – you know it's seventy paces to the studio? Well, it is. And when I got there, I put my hand on the door handle. I couldn't face it. I had to turn back. I just couldn't face it.

How often does that happen?

Oh, it can happen. I got scared . . . You're not writing this down, are you? [*Laughing.*]

You can tell me not to. But it seems to be part of the process. We were going to talk about your progress in writing the piece.

It never occurred to me it was interesting.

It's to do with how you're getting on.

Oh, I see. Well, I got to the point of putting the key in the door and then I stopped. I turned back. Came back inside the house. And I made some phone calls, then I . . . This is very pseud. I just happened to be in the bathroom and I read some of that American woman . . . What's she called?

Emily Dickinson?

Emily Dickinson. Correct. I read some Emily Dickinson contemplating my navel with my Japanese kit on! [*Laughing.*] I like wearing it. I'll tell you what it's good for. See this pocket here – I can put my glasses in it. Perfect. Though my glasses aren't in it now. Oh no. I don't know where they are.

So it's not for the local tai chi class?

Oh God . . . no way.

Then what happened? You went back, you made yourself sit down?

I went back, walked my seventy paces again. And this time I went into the studio, I sat down and started trying not to panic. I prevaricated. Or procrastinated. And, um [*long pause*], I wrote the first thing that came into my head.

And?

Then I contemplated it for a long time. And tried to think how I could do something, proliferate the idea . . . the stuttering musical thought I was trying to express. Then I worked out something quite intricate and then I made a relationship between two rhythmic parts. A rhythmic process. And I thought about it.

That took the whole morning.

Did you stop panicking?

I'm still panicking. I am. Honestly. It's a sort of cross between depression and panic. The question is, what am I going to do? Very often the decisions are made not in the quality of the material I generate. It's how I feel about it. It's not about its quality. I'm sure if I were in a different frame of mind I'd think it was really rather interesting.

So that's the answer. I'm afraid I haven't got anything else to say today. Unless you've got some questions.

Perhaps it's part of the whole question of how the audience for a piece of music or work of art cannot tell what went into making in. And art is not always better for being the result of enormous or prolonged effort. It can be as powerful even if achieved quickly.

Yes. And as I may have said already, there are certain wounds that I feel exist in pieces I've written and then they disappear. Or I know there have been difficulties in something and then they are forgotten. Or I can't remember what they are. When they play the piece there isn't a red light that goes on that indicates 'this was a difficult bit'.

This snag in the process of writing – has it delayed your nominal three pages a week?

Oh, I'm not worried about that. I've lost track.

So you're panicking but you're not worried?

There are two things about duration. One is whether you've got time to do it, and I certainly have. The other is the way it's progressing. If it's progressing the way it should, I've got time to do it. You see?

I'd like it to be twenty-five minutes of music because that's very often how long it takes pieces to speak.

How much do you think you've got now?

I don't know. I'm trying not to think about it. I'm trying to listen to it – where I am in the journey.

So you've got a sense of the whole piece, and the scale of it, but you don't know where you are in it?

Well, I know where I am with what I've done, and what form it is. It's not to do with external, pre-compositional architecture. I've learned to trust my – this horrible word again – my creativity. I know more or less how I want the piece to speak. So we'll see.

[Long, very long, silence.]

Let's try a simpler topic. How did your visit with the guitarist for your new piece go?

We've got to do this right. It's an interesting story. Have we talked about it before?

Yes, a bit . . . Try it again.

It's quite good to put it on record and get the chronology right. Julian Bream lives near me. I've met him from time to time over the years. We used to play cricket. He had a team. I used to play for the other side.

Batsman? Or bowler?

I'm a bowler. Was.

So I met him once a year. It was the peasants versus the artists. I always played for the peasants. It's just how it worked out. Once I got hit in the balls. Do you know what that's like?

No, actually . . .

It's the worst pain I've ever encountered. Unbelievable. Anyway you don't need to write that down.

And then we used to meet in Waitrose in Gillingham [Dorset]. He – Julian – goes there too.

So we have had a long-standing ongoing conversation about how he had some fantastic wine from 1961 – and he would always tell me about this wine. And as the years went by I'd say, 'How is the wine coming on, Julian?'

Then two years ago or so, he said, 'I'm leaving my house' – he had a beautiful manor farm and he was moving somewhere smaller – and he gave me a case of twelve bottles of this amazing 1961 claret. And maybe it was a hundred years too old but it was a great wine . . . And a wonderful act of generosity.

Anyway, it all developed our relationship and led to him wanting me to write a piece. He has a foundation and commissions music though maybe he wouldn't automatically go for the kind of thing I do. He puts a concert on every two years in the Wigmore Hall. And he asked me if I'd do something, which really sealed our relationship. We have the same birthday. He's a year older. I'm going to his eightieth next week.

So the idea was that I would write it and he would go through it with me and tell me what was impossible to play – because I hadn't written much for the instrument and didn't really know the idiom. So it was a first throw of the dice.

So I wrote a section and took it to him but I didn't really want what he was suggesting.

That's probably inevitable given that it's your piece . . .

Yes. All I wanted was to know was if the chords were playable.

What were his comments?

Well, he had suggestions that perhaps would have made it nicer than I wanted it to be. Adding a particular note to a chord for example, whereas I wanted sparseness – that sort of thing.

Then he wrote to me and said he thought he was too old. He didn't use the word reactionary – which he isn't, anyway – but some word like that – to deal with what I was writing.

Which is touching given he is only one year older than you . . .

So I wrote the whole piece and sent it to Jonathan Leath-wood. Well, you were here when I rang him up and then when he rang me back. And he said there was no problem with any of it!

So now Julian has written a nice letter saying he's pleased with it and he knows it must have been 'half a nightmare in the daytime' to write for guitar! He's very knowledgeable and has wonderful, exceptional ears for music. I just think maybe he has reservations about mine.

So anyway, Jonathan came here and he was going to come with Julian. But Julian then had a doctor's appointment, or something like that, and was going to come later. Then I got a call saying could I take Jonathan over to his house instead, because his dog is black . . . [*Laughing.*]

What do you mean, his dog is black?

He said I can't come over because the dog is black.

What dog?

His dog. He's got this bloody great dog.

But what's wrong with it being black?

Apparently it's black and it absorbs the sun and gets too hot so he couldn't take it for a walk so had to stay home . . . [*Laughing.*] I don't know what he was going on about but

[170]

his reason was that the weather was too hot and the dog was black and I said, 'Julian, what do you mean . . . the dog's black?' That was why he didn't come. Unless I got the wrong end of the stick.

So Jonathan came over here and played the whole piece. We went through it section by section and he made some very good suggestions. He even suggested it could be more difficult. I asked what he meant. He showed me what he meant and I said, well, I don't write music to be difficult, only to be more like itself.

What did he suggest?

Oh, things like harmonics. The fundamental problem about the guitar – I've said this before and it seems very obvious but it's the essence of writing for the instrument – is that if you stop a note, when you move from it, it can't resonate. It's not like a violin with a bow or a piano with a pedal.

One of the other difficulties is trying not to go for notes that are open strings. Then you get too much repetition as there are only six strings!

So that's the sort of thing Jonathan dealt with and played it potentially brilliantly and was very clear in a way that Julian – well, I don't know, I wasn't getting quite the same from him. Jonathan gave me exactly what I needed.

Nothing normalised what I was doing . . . I said the whole nature of this piece is in the false relations which are sounded at the beginning of the piece. I want the sound of the fifths and the tritones at the start. That's what the piece is about. I don't want it to be enriched or made nice.

[171]

So we went through it and then went to take it over to Julian. It was about 6 p.m. by then. We went over to his house and Jonathan played through it for him and Julian was wonderful, and suddenly getting quite technical. It showed instantly what an amazing musician he is. They were talking absolutely technically – if you play that note with that fingering, etc., etc. He kept asking me if it would be all right and I didn't have a clue what they were talking about so I said, 'Play it for me, what you're suggesting and I'll tell you whether it's all right. Don't tell me what finger you're playing it with because I don't care!'

A lot of questions cropped up about this open harmony. I didn't want it filled in. And about halfway through Julian saw what I was after. His natural twitch would be to make it richer and my twitch would be to keep it more open. And he got that.

So Jonathan Leathwood is the right person for the piece?

Oh, he's terrific.

What's the piece called?

'Beyond the White Hand'.

Meaning?

I wrote a piece for Silas called *Guitar and White Hand*. It's a reference to a picture by Picasso. You know the thing about Picasso and the guitar – he was obsessed by it, and the idea that the shape was like a woman. He did loads. But my favourite is the cardboard one.

[Harry fetches the exhibition catalogue *Picasso: Guitars 1912–14* by Anne Umland, Museum of Modern Art, New York, 2011.]

You know it was sent to MOMA in New York in a packet, in flat pieces of cardboard. They tried to assemble it and there was one piece that didn't fit . . . it's a great story, told in this catalogue. The piece they couldn't work out was a table for the guitar to sit on! But that's another matter . . .

They're all collages. And he did a drawing, like a child's cut-out, labelling what colours each piece should be. I don't know whether you can express colours in music – I'm rather against it. But I thought to write a sort of deconstructed piece based on it. It's as if you'd cut out all the pieces and coloured them and put it together again.

So you were going to write a different piece for each colour?

Yes, but I found I didn't want to write a suite of colours! So I wrote sections which correspond to these colours, in this big piece. But I put them in a way that Picasso might have done, using a collage effect. Not doing a bit that's blue and a bit that's pink but making it all into one piece. Does that make sense?

Here [in the catalogue] are the colours: rose, bleu, jaune, blanc, gris, noir . . .

[173]

So I'm having a go at a similar idea a hundred years later. My piece is a sort of homage. I wrote out the words, *rose, bleu, jaune* . . . I wrote separate pieces called those names and I subjected them to a collage . . . and . . . um . . .

You seem tired. Do you want to stop?

Up to you. We can go on.

When I spoke to Silas he was interested that you are described as writing 'English music', and felt that no one had really delved fully into what that means. Either for you or in terms of the music . . . He felt that there were so many aspects of your work which are to do with landscape, especially the English landscape. He quoted you as saying you could work in a concrete bunker but clearly the places you've lived or come across have mattered to you. Can we tackle that? He felt he hadn't really worked out that aspect of you . . .

Well, I don't know whether I have. [*Chuckles.*] I'm in the process of doing it.

But it's a real question. What could be more landscape-driven and in a sense English than Silbury Air?

OK. It's a serious point. If you go to Berlin there's a labyrinth to the Holocaust – the white stones. I didn't know what it was. And I said to a woman, 'What is it?' She said, 'It's *obvious* what it is.' And I said, 'Well, you tell me. I don't know. How would I know?'

It only becomes about that subject when you see the title.

Did you know Penderecki wrote a piece about Hiroshima [*Threnody for the Victims of Hiroshima*, 1960] – famous string piece. The point being, it had an ordinary title, or no title, and the conductor suggested he called it that. And it assumes that meaning, it becomes poetically charged because of the title.

So to come back to my interest in landscape and how it reflects, this is not in a mysterious, mystical way. But there's a magical quality when things have secrets, and it's the mystery you never want to have explained. I lose interest when I get the explanation. It's like sculpture when the arms are missing –

The Venus de Milo?

Yes. I'm saying it has a mystery for the very fact of missing something, or being in a sense unknowable. It gains something by what is absent.

How does that relate to place?

That piece there – the guitar piece with the colours – it's all present at the same time. I had to, as it were, make a landscape of that deconstruction.

Silbury for me is all about the mystery of not knowing what it is. There's a formality about it. It's like making an object and taking the title away.

Oh God, I can't explain it but I feel so strongly about it.

One of my favourite places round here is an Iron Age circle on Whitesheet Hill. No one knows anything about it. If it turned out to have a mundane practical meaning I'd be terribly disappointed. I want it to be –

Arcane?

That's it. You've got the word! Arcane. *Arcana*. Akani. Akela. Wasn't that what they had at Cubs? [*Laughing.*]
   For me, it's my circle. It has a mystery.

Is that true of, say, the Green Knight too?

I think so. If we knew exactly what it was for or why it was there, it would be less interesting. It's elemental, something that's always been around.

If someone says 'pagan' does that have a resonance for you?

Yes. It's to do with another side of making imagery, like the carved leaves of Southwell Minster. It's not just about the glory of God, it's about the glory of nature.
   One of the nicest things I've ever seen were the trees inside Westminster Abbey for the last wedding of whoever it was [*Prince William and Catherine Middleton*]. Did you go to it?

No, I didn't, Harry!

Nor did I. Just watched it on telly. It was completely staggering. Did you see that? Whoever hit on the idea of having these big trees inside the abbey really hit on something. It was completely logical. The trees became formal, and as if part of the building. It was not commented on by anyone as far as I know but then I don't read all that crap.

So it's the formalisation that counts. If pushed, that's how I feel about landscape. I'm not trying to express rolling hills or a green and pleasant land or northern gruffness, you know?

Northern gruffness?

I don't think I am northern gruff. But I think some people would like me to be . . . To go back to this Picasso picture – it's a deconstructed guitar. Let's look at it again. Sketchbook. Guitar. Spring/Summer 1913. A hundred and two drawings. Ink and pencil on graph paper. Coloured paper. Wallpaper cover. Well that's exactly a hundred years ago and now I'm doing mine . . .

You have talked about the landscape in France being hard, without soil.

It was '*causses*' – a flat, arid crust, completely barren.

You had a studio there that you built . . .

I wrote *Gawain* there.

Only Gawain?

And *Secret Theatre.*

We can talk about this more another time . . .

Have I told you, drystone walling is a thing of mine? I come from there. That's what I grew up with. I used to mend drystone walls. I learned how to do it with a friend in Scotland. It's a very interesting thing. You have a random pile of stones and the people who can really do it never pick up a stone and put it back in the pile. They look at the space and then find a piece to put there.

What you or I would do is look at the pile and think now where could I put that? And then we'd put it back and try another. My father told me that. I find that interesting.

Look at this crap here [*indicating garden wall*] – this is not stone. It's reconstituted and there are just five shapes.

But that bit there [*points to a lower wall nearer the house*], isn't that lovely? The boy who made that died, very soon afterwards and unexpectedly. He was very innocent, and a slightly rough customer. He'd never done it before and he loved doing it.

11 July 2013

THE MET OFFICE HAS DECLARED THIS IS OFFICIALLY
A HEATWAVE. ROADS ARE MELTING, TREES SUFFERING
FROM 'SUMMER BRANCH DROP', EMERGENCY SERVICES
OVERWORKED. TEMPERATURE 30+ DEGREES.

Harry is glued to the cricket, England vs Australia, the first match of the Ashes. To the world's amazement and Harry's delight, the nineteen-year-old Australian left-arm spinner Ashton Agar, a surprise selection, has just scored a sparkling 98, the best ever performance by a no. 11 batsman in a Test match.

Today Harry is wearing a full kimono. The old plum tree is laden with a surreal bounty of hard fruit in clusters, now more like grapes than the little olives of a few weeks ago. The quince trees are dotted with immature green fruit — and the fig, too, for the first time in Harry's memory. He spends a long time opening elaborate packets of tea bought in Japan, stirring the pot with a delicate, split-bamboo whisk, retrieved from a tailor-made container and replaced, carefully, after use. 'Beautiful, isn't it? Bamboo. You make the tea frothy, like an espresso.' He serves a Japanese sweet wrapped up in several layers and tasting of nothing but sweetness. Did he know what he was purchasing? No. 'I just liked the packets. They left them in the hotel room.' A desultory conversation about tea is played out to its last variation. A full eight minutes into the recording he is still making, stirring, pouring tea and unwrapping the sweets.

Can we start? Are you ready?

[Big sigh.]

We can try. Suppose so. Have you got any questions?

You began to say, when I arrived –

Forgotten.

– something about the title of the guitar piece –

Oh yes. I've changed it. The title. I've found one that's more apt. And which relates more to Picasso. It's this one here. It's called *Construction with Guitar Player*. That's what the painting is called. For me, it describes the process of the piece. Julian wasn't terribly convinced. He didn't like the word construction. I rang him to tell him. He wanted something softer.

One of the nice things is that there's humour – the arm, and the real guitar, it's very funny. Completely potty. It's a journey between reality and fantasy. The reality is the table with the drink. Funny in a way music can't be. I don't see how music can be humorous.

Ever?

The only music I think is truly funny is Rossini. And it's always the same joke.

Not Haydn?

Well, it's a bit contrived, isn't it?

Kagel?

Oh, he's not funny. Do you think he is? Some people do . . .

Where did your interest in Picasso start?

Well, I was a bit disappointed in Klee. I found far more connection with Picasso. He embodies all the things I'd want to be. He's on the side of Dionysus much more than Apollo. Braque was the Apollonian. It's a question of quantity. It's not that there's no lyrical side to Picasso.

So you imply that you are more Dionysian.

I am very conscious of being pretentious. I can't use the word. But then I'm so self-conscious about all that stuff. I can't even find a word for 'creativity'. *[Laughing.]*

But if, instead, I use the word 'Dionysian' about you, will you accept that applies to you? And if so, how would you put its meaning into words? Maybe people have a better understanding of the concept of 'Apollonian' . . .

Well, Stravinsky had it too. The Dionysus thing. It's harder edged. It has classical implications. The question of construction and form is central . . . I'm not thinking very well. To make formal music without it being formalistic . . . Does that make sense? I don't think I'm being any good today . . . I'm sure I'm going stupid.

It's not an easy thing to express . . . at 4 p.m. on a sweltering afternoon . . .

There's a sort of formality which I had in the back of my mind, that has an arcane quality. It's formal but that formality is hidden. You can't analyse or explain it. If I was in a good mood I could talk about this. It's about mystery.

I've never wanted to write music that relates to anything apart from itself.

You know there are composers who can't make a move without it relating to something historically.

You mean musical?

Yes. An example might be [Thomas] Adès – this is an observation not a criticism – nearly everything relates to something else, a model.

You are trying to write music without any model? You are making your own forms?

But it always has to have its own internal logic. I'm talking about orchestral or instrumental pieces. Music without texts. That's the interesting thing about *Mask of Orpheus*. The narrative is a foregone conclusion . . . It assumes a knowledge of the narrative because it's so simple. So you can assume the journey of the narrative and forget about it. You don't have to throw your obsessions – another word I can't deal with – at it. You can use your intuition as you would in a piece of orchestral music. You're free, in a way you aren't usually with text-based pieces.

If I had another lifetime I'd explore that idea further . . .

The *Symphonies of Wind Instruments* is always the model I come back to.

What did you mean about Braque?

They seem similar. But you can tell the difference immediately when you look at them, they embody opposite sides. You might say Braque invented cubism and Picasso played with it. You could say he pushed it so hard so as to destroy it in a way. It's like a child having a toy – Picasso would always destroy it in the end.

And you said you wanted to talk about Brancusi.

Yes. No. Not particularly.

I've misunderstood . . .

No. Brancusi does have a quality that, dare I say, I identify with . . . That's horrible, isn't it? [*Laughing.*] Pseud's Corner.

But you're allowed to identify with someone without it being Pseud's Corner material.

You've seen that picture of him with that big saw? That's what I identify with! What? The rough with the smooth. That simplicity. He's carving the 'Endless Column' [*Column of the Infinite*].

That's why I'm having trouble with my work at the moment. I think that simplicity is something you earn. You can't just do something simple. I feel more and more attracted to, or that I'm moving towards, a sense of directness. But it's also impossible.

Is it a directness that –

I don't know. I haven't done it yet, darlin'! *[Laughing.]* But I was working towards it in that piece you didn't hear – *In Broken Images*. It's dangerously, to me, transparent.

You mean as in the whiteness you describe in the guitar piece?

That sort of thing.

I think the juxtapositions of material in the guitar piece are dangerous. It's the same old bloody question. You've got stuff at the back of your head and finding the way of expressing it . . .

It's very easy to smooth the edges.

Will any of these changes in your attitude, almost a distillation of everything you've done to this point, be audible to the listener? Or at least a listener who knows other music of yours?

I don't know.

[Extremely long silence.]

I wrote *In Broken Images* under very difficult circumstances.

When Sheila was dying?

Yes.

The decisions I made, in getting from one element to the next, in the construction – I don't want them to be obvious. And yet at the same time you lose the nature of the material by not being obvious. That's my neurosis . . .

That's your neurosis?

Oh, I don't know what we're talking about! It can't be simplistic – that's my worry.

Look at Brancusi's 'Endless Column'. I can do that. The only difference between me and him is that he did it. Yet that mark that he cuts with the chisel, he hasn't chiselled it out and made it subtle. It's the most extreme example. The only thing you could do that would be more extreme would be just to have a piece of wood sticking out of the ground.

If I did something like that I'd think, if you're looking up at it it'll seem as if it's tapering. And I'd want to do something – make each one [rhomboid] slightly bigger on the repeat so that when you looked at it you would think it was right and yet you'd have the strange illusion that it's all the same size, which it isn't. That's the kind of thing I'd get up to. And the sort of thing I'd be neurotic about – getting it right.

Why do you use the word 'neurotic'?

Because I couldn't just leave it, like he did. I've only just thought of that. If I were doing something as direct as that I'd think wouldn't it be an interesting idea to make it so it doesn't taper . . . ? I'm giving you this as an example of what took place at the second when I looked at it and thought, 'I could do that.' Then my mind started whirring.

That's your spatial imagination . . . Maybe you are countering what you think of as your dyslexia with an over-active spatial awareness? It's often the way you talk about your music.

Yes, but I'm talking about how I think of an interesting thing and make it more complicated. Not that I have any intention of doing it . . . !

But you're doing a similar thing in the piano concerto – when you talked about doubling the speed of an idea but keeping the tempo the same?

Yes, exactly.

Would you like to stop now?

I'm exhausted.

17 July 2013

Harry has had his seventy-ninth birthday since we met. He celebrated it with a lunch for family and friends in a neighbourhood restaurant he particularly likes, near Toby's house in East London. When I arrive he is reading *Ill Met by Moonlight* by W. Stanley Moss, in a well-preserved orange-and-cream Penguin paperback. Published in 1950, it relates the author's and Patrick Leigh Fermor's escapades in Crete during the Second World War as agents for the Special Operations Executive (SOE). 'Toby gave it to me. I sort of knew Patrick Leigh Fermor. I'm interested in this stuff.'

Because of the heat, from which Harry is suffering greatly, we move location and, for the first time, sit at the other end of the house, which is cool and dark, and dominated by books – on art, birds, wild flowers, gardening, cooking, wine, but few on music. The walls are bold: a raspberry-terracotta distemper. A red stencilled border round the door, painted by Harry himself, suggests Japanese style. There's a television. A big monochrome picture of a pig by Adam Birtwistle hangs on the far wall, one of well over a dozen by Adam around the house.

From across the room this pig picture has the appearance of an eighteenth-century engraving. In fact it's a pen-and-ink wash in shades of dark and light grey. Beneath, on a chest, stands a pink plaster pig, also by Adam and testament to

Harry's father's pig-farming days. It is like a hard, expression-ist version of a child's money-box pig, but still amiable.

For no particular reason Harry brings out a pair of knitted socks with toes like gloves from Japan, and starts laughing. 'For my feet! They gave them to me as a present. What will I do with them?' There is no tea ceremony or kimono today.

You've had a birthday. And also attended Julian Bream's eightieth . . .

He dislikes my title.

[The discussion appears to have been quite heated near the end of the party. Harry is unwilling to say exactly what happened, but agrees they had words.]

So what will you do about the title?

Keep it.

Since they provoke such a reaction, we had better discuss titles.

I think I'm quite good at titles. I got two by accident from Robert Graves. *In Broken Images* and *Secret Theatre*.

Secret Theatre was going to be called 'Mystery Play'. I came across this poem. It's not just a better title. It's a more precise description of the piece, or at least it is in the opening lines. Something about a flute sounding – and that's how the piece starts, though I'd already written it when I found the poem:

When from your sleepy mind the day's burden
Falls like a bushel sack on a barn floor,
Be prepared for music, for natural mirages
And for the night's incomparable parade of colour.

It is hours after midnight now, a flute signals
Far off; we mount the stage as though at random
Boldly ring down the curtain, then dance out our love.
[from 'Secret Theatre' by Robert Graves]

That sofa next door belonged to Robert Graves. The one with
the leopard-skin material, though it didn't come like that.

How?

His son lived next to us. His first wife gave it to us and she
said it was Robert's. In Anstey Combe [Wiltshire] – years
ago. We had a rather gingerbread cottage with a thatch and
it had been underpinned. I remember Sam Graves saying his
father, who was very tall, could kick the ceiling in that house
because it was so low . . .

[The sofa story peters out.]

What about Endless Parade? An Imaginary Landscape?

My titles. I write the piece and then find the title, usually.
The best titles are oxymorons. What's an oxymoron? Do I
mean oxymoron? *Still Movement*. That's a good title but a
bad piece. My best title is *The Axe Manual* – a piece I wrote

for Emanuel Ax. *Air* is a play on air and air. *Grimethorpe Aria* is an anti-brass band piece. In a sense it's a landscape piece. It's that sort of Yorkshire mining landscape . . . It's a melancholy work.

Triumph of Time is from a picture. *Exody* is in the dictionary but it's a Robin Blaser poem. *Carmen arcadiae mechanicae perpetuum* – I gave the title I wanted to [the poet and classicist] Tony Harrison in English and said put it into Latin. Then *Panic*, at least to me, is onomatopoeic.

Has anyone until now ever objected to your titles?

No. I've even been complimented on them.

Are there any others taken from pictures?

Yes, *Melencolia*.

That's you . . .

Yes, it is. Though it's after Dürer. Piece for clarinet and orchestra. They're playing it next year.

Are there other pieces you are glad are being revisited in your eightieth-birthday year?

No. I don't want to hear any of them.

Is that really true?

Mm. Yeah. Partly true.

Do you sometimes feel you want to hear them? You enjoyed hearing Exody *in Japan.*

Well, I didn't want to hear it. But it was the first time I'd really heard it properly. I'd forgotten I'd done anything like that.

Do other pieces bring out that feeling in you — of hearing something you hadn't realised you'd written?

How can I describe to you . . . ? I approach them with caution and trepidation. Very often, I've talked about this, I know there are wounds . . . Sometimes, perhaps it's just the performance, pieces work better.

So that probably is largely the performance?

I'm scared to death hearing this opera [*Gawain*, the opening opera in the Salzburg Festival 2013], next week or whenever it is.

Because you haven't heard it since it was last done?

Mm. Yeah.

What does 'scared to death' mean in this context? It'll keep you awake . . . ?

Yeah. Keep me awake. But not so much that. More that everything's wrong.

Why?

That my life is a total waste of time, a failure.

So your opera is being done in Salzburg, one of the highest-profile music events in the world, and you're saying you are a total waste of time?

Mm.

You don't think that's a contradiction? It may be how you feel but it's not how others see it . . .

I'm not looking forward to it. If I could get out of it, I would.

Don't you feel like that about every piece of yours you are about to hear?

No.

And it's not about what you've heard about the production? The dog, the Joseph Beuys concept?

No. Nothing to do with that. Though it sounds pretty terrible. I don't care about the production as long as the performance is good. They tell me the cast is very very good. If it's any good musically you don't have to watch. Don't you think?

Fair enough. But if the music is well done, and you are not worried about the production, surely it's a given. You know the piece well enough . . .

Some of it will be all right.

So you must regard next year with some dread?

Yeah.
    Weighed in the balance and found wanting.

Don't you think, perhaps, you've gone past that point?

Have I?

Your reputation is established for your lifetime. You've got the grand status?

Have I?

Posterity will make its own decision.

It doesn't get any better. I know what I think. In the end, there's only the work. And I can't help what I feel about it. It's like having a target. You can see it. You know where you want the arrow to go.
    I'm being absolutely truthful.

You'd probably stop writing if you didn't feel that in some way? You'd be resting on laurels.

I'd just be writing another piece. I know how to write a certain type of music. I don't want to write it.

You want to do something new?

It's not about being new . . .

I'm having a real struggle writing this piano piece. I'm doing something rather interesting, really. And the fact that it is the way it is, it can easily fail.

But you'll try and eventually succeed?

It's caused me a lot of trouble. I think I'll be all right. There'll be some interesting things in it.

You haven't gone to the studio door and turned away again?

No. Well, yeah, a bit.

Not as bad as the day last week?

No, not quite as bad as that.

You see, for instance, I'm doing something which seemed very straightforward right now. I knew that in order to do it I simply had to mechanically go through what is going on. But the problem with writing music is that it takes such a long time. You think, that mechanism, if I keep going on, it'll be terrible. I have to fight my instinct to change it and develop it. That's not what I'm aiming at. I mustn't do it. I must stick to my guns. The piano keeps playing the same thing – just a bar of five beats. But in between are what I call windows.

I call them windows because they're periods of varying lengths in between what the piano does, which is always the same. Obstinately the same. What happens in the windows always triggers something, then it stops. So it's a series of seven windows.

That's difficult. Just to write it out, and believe in it. The 'tic' is that I wanted to change it all the time. But the longer I can wait, the last time it happens – this piano figure – it's suddenly going to continue. Rhythmically it's the same but I have made tiny, subtle changes but you wouldn't know unless you kept hearing it. Like putting a slightly different shadow on something . . .

This motif happens seven times.

Seven times because it's a significant number in some way?

No. It just seemed to be right.

Have you finished that section?

No. I'm still doing it. I keep saying to myself, 'Now listen here, Harry. Just stick to your guns.' It's like having a [stage] curtain which shuts, then plays rather banal stuff, then you open it and the idea is there again, subtly different.

Did you know you would be doing that in this piece? When you started?

No. Yes. Once I'd made that decision, on one level it's so obvious you can't make it subtle. The subtlety is somewhere else.

How far into it are you?

Half.

So ten minutes?

Yes.

So you have to finish these seven repetitions you've described and then carry on – all before you go on your travels next week?

No, I won't manage that. But I'm not worried about it.

You have an idea for the next bit? But you may not do what you think, today, you are likely to do.

It happens to me all the time. I think I know what I'm going to do next. But I bet I don't. Let's come back to that!

The piano so far is all questions, short things. I know I've got to the point where the piano has to have a substantial part, where the relationship between soloist and orchestra is different. It's got to be freer, expansive, more like a slow movement. It's got to be five minutes. It'll be thinner, more like chamber music. I can introduce linear ideas, with the woodwind . . .

One thing that makes it easier is that because I've been feeling my way in the dark, the fumbling becomes form. And

I just hope that if I can get there, there's a form and it will become clear.

Then there's got to be an ending.

Do you think you've got a puritanical streak in you? Working. You're pretty strict with yourself.

I think I'm hanging on with my fingers at the edge of the cliff. And if I let go . . .

Doesn't anyone making anything feel like that?

I don't know.

So if you stop you'll be in the chasm?

Yes.

I feel that what I'm doing now is living dangerously. When I wrote my songs – for Mark Padmore – I felt I was in a sense very much in control. I can play the piano well enough so I can hear. The material is clear enough to know exactly that it will work.

Here I'm doing something else. It's got its origin in the other piece – *In Broken Images* – the way the piece works.

But it's complex. And the complexity is not to do with figuration though it's very intricate. In the way that it speaks, I don't know how it will work. It isn't easy.

I want to write a piece called *Deep Time*. Sombre piece. Half an hour. For Barenboim. I can see a way of doing it. It's the last big piece I'll do. Maybe.

This is gloomy – not the idea of the piece but the way you are talking about it . . . Here's a gear switch . . .

Go on then. See if you can.

You're about to spend time with David Harsent, in Salzburg. And he is currently working on the text of your new theatre piece, The Cure. *He said something in Aldeburgh which I wanted to check with you: that you had said you could not set the words 'underpass' or 'fuck' . . .*

I can't.

Why not?

Because I wouldn't know how to make a context, vocally. Something like that. It would be incongruous. I have some contemporary poems I was thinking of setting but they – the poems – suddenly start swearing – and that's fine on the page but in music you need a totally different style of language. You'd have to be like a sort of punk or something.

I don't think of you as very punk.

No, I'm not very punk. [*Laughing.*] Definitely not very punk.

29 July 2013

SALZBURG, AUSTRIA. TEMPERATURE 37 DEGREES:
STEAMY AND STULTIFYING.

Harry is sitting on the terrace in a humdrum tourist hotel on the edge of the city, where he is staying, reading a Cézanne biography by Philip Callow and looking as if he is melting. A party of students from the Far East is making a raucous noise in the lobby. Silas and a friend of his from London are there. Harry finds the heat intolerable. The opening night of *Gawain* has taken place. It has been well received, though Harry and David Harsent dislike the production intensely.

On the way to a rehearsal that afternoon of an instrumental concert of his music, Harry comes across a small commercial gallery in Salzburg that has an exhibition of Picasso ceramics and drawings, including subjects that relate directly to Harry's work: bull, minotaur, guitar, Pan figures. He particularly likes a plate with ochre glaze depicting a bull in the style of the Lascaux cave paintings – after visiting them in 1940, Picasso reportedly remarked, 'We have learned nothing.'

You were dreading coming here. You hate the production but the music has survived brilliantly intact. Are you ready to talk about it – how it's going? The second performance of Gawain *is today . . .*

The worst thing almost has been the heat. Yesterday I thought this is what dying must be like. Seriously. Hearing the piece was very memorable. There's hardly a moment I didn't remember. I find it interesting how music fits into the memory – but I've said that before. I've talked about discovering, recently, a great interest in Schumann – appreciating it more. I feel like that about a lot of classical music – and I don't go to many concerts. I come across music rather than go in search of it.

Hearing it as an instrumental player in an orchestra is a funny position to be in. You don't really get the whole piece. The perspective is all different. You're just a cog. When I was in Scotland and France I heard very little music. Then I came back and started hearing a few more concerts. I heard Adrian Brendel and his father play the Beethoven cello sonatas and somehow I knew every single note. I don't know how. God knows where that came from.

All through our conversations you keep going back to Beethoven. I was speaking to Mitsuko Uchida, for whom you wrote another piano and orchestra work, Antiphonies. *She brought up the subject of Beethoven's Fourth Piano Concerto, which you have mentioned. She pointed out moments of repetition where he won't give up. Mozart, she noted, would have been far too impatient and had several different ideas in the intervening bars. But Beethoven is obstinate, unyielding. All that tallied with the repeated idea you were discussing in the UK last week. And here we are in the city of Mozart . . .*

I'm more and more struck by the journey of the music of Beethoven. I get the feeling with Mozart that he would write, maybe, an exposition in the morning and if it didn't work he'd write another in the afternoon. There's a logical inevitability about Mozart's music, even in the more obscure works like the *Jupiter* Symphony, No. 41 – a very strange piece. My understanding is that it's baroque in the sense that the gesture goes more or less where you expect it to whereas in Beethoven it doesn't and I'm struck by that more and more.

I identify with certain things. I'm not saying I'm Beethoven or anything silly like that. But I'm conscious of how he gets out of situations. In one, you slowly dissolve and it becomes something new. In others you just stop and do something else. I find myself listening to that logic.

I like Mitsuko a lot. I wrote *Antiphonies* for her originally but she was ill. Eventually she played it in Los Angeles. I don't know what she thought of it . . .

What she said was that sometimes you had written fff *for the piano and she had said, 'Harry, if you really want the piano to be heard here you must write a triple* pianissimo, *not a triple* forte'*!*

I don't like the piece.

You say that about most of your pieces.

Yes, I know.

It's a work for piano and orchestra . . . a concerto? Not a concerto?

What's the difference? I'm writing another to get it right . . .

[201]

[Pause.]

Oh Christ, it's the bloody sun coming out again. Don't want that.

Tell me more about Gawain. *Last week you wanted to be saved from coming here* . . .

Yeah.

Now you're here . . .

Yeah. What's the question?

This is a conversation. Not a set of questions. But OK, are you prepared to say how you are really finding it?

It's not why I wrote the opera – to be put in a visual and dramatic language that uses one idea to explain another. It would have been much better to write a new piece for the production! There's no match.

Isn't it the age-old problem of a work being out in the world and then taken up and shaped by an interpreter?

I've always said that when you do a thing for the first time it's got to be close to what the composer wrote the piece for. Then in future there can be more experimentation. But there's still got to be some logic. You can do it under the water, in the sea, in a lunatic asylum. Do we still say lunatic asylum? But you've still got to tell the story, and make the narrative clear. But when it's perverted . . .

So you're saying the narrative here in the Salzburg production is perverted?

Well, if someone is saying something and doing another I'd have thought that was perverted, isn't it?

Does that make you angry, or upset?

Oh, I think my reaction is very complicated. I'm not sure what I think. I think the piece is strong enough . . .

That's a good outcome in one way?

It's a negative in a way. For all that, musically the performance is very very good. I talked to the singers, who love singing it, which is something because I was born into a world where you weren't supposed to write what they considered 'modern' music for the voice.

And I talked to the orchestra too. And they said they loved doing it. They're happy. And as with singers, I was born into a world where getting orchestras to play 'my' sort of music was like trying to get children to eat cabbage.

One remark I found rewarding was that Alexander Pereira [Artistic Director, Salzburg Festival] was talking about other operas which sounded dated to the time they were written – he gave some examples, I can't remember what they were, from the 1970s and 1980s. But he said this one seemed absolutely timeless – musically and in subject matter – which meant a good deal to me.

That's pleasing.

Oh yeah – if it's true. You can't sit down and write timeless music. It is what it is. I don't know what I'm doing and I have no control over it.

There's something in this [Cézanne] book I'm reading – a Leonardo quote: 'Art lives by constraints and dies of freedom.'

A different take on 'Man is born free and everywhere is in chains'...

It makes the point clearly. Both comments do.

You could say you have come out of the Salzburg experience well.

I've got away with it. That's what I feel. I've think I've probably got away with it. Maybe.

So can you afford to be a little less hard on yourself?

I'm no more hard on myself than with any other piece I listen to. I'm very encouraged, if you like, about the vocal music – I was talking to the tenor, Andrew Watts, who was Bishop Baldwin in *Gawain*. It expresses the text. It's essentially for a lyric voice, even when it's angry. It's concerned with line. I'm talking about the things I strive to achieve. I think it works in that sense.

I know you were, understandably, full of apprehension –

Not more than about anything else.

But was it about hearing Gawain?

I hadn't heard it for a long time. Didn't know what it was. The game is bigger than listening to a string trio. They're doing, this evening, *Verses for Ensembles*. I really don't want to hear that. I really don't. I'm not scared or anything. But it's a piece unlike any other.

But you've heard it plenty of times.

Oh, lots of times. Hundreds of times. I wrote it for the London Sinfonietta in 1968–9 – the second piece they played. First was a piece by John Tavener, then this. I remember when we were discussing the idea they said shall we have lunch – David Atherton, Tony Pay, Nicholas Snowman. And I said yes, there's a restaurant I like in Charlotte Street . . . French . . .

L'Etoile?

Yes. L'Etoile. Used to be a brothel. There was a waiter who cut up chicken a certain way and always told the same joke. Years later I went back and he was still telling exactly the same joke. And there was a mad wine waiter. I got to know him quite well. Then years later, I was walking late one night near the bus station at Victoria, and I saw a dishevelled man pushing a pram with all his worldly belongings in and I said, 'I know you. You're the wine waiter at L'Etoile . . .' And it was.

Anyway. The point is the lunch cost more than their whole season's concert budget. [*Laughing.*]

[Three statuesque blond Bavarians squeeze past the table gesturing and chattering loudly.]

Rhine maidens . . . All Rhine maidens . . .

Later that day in Salzburg I have arranged to have lunch with John Tomlinson, the British bass who has created two roles for Harry. By chance he was born in the same nursing home in Accrington as Harry, twelve years later. He has achieved international fame in the role of Wagner's Wotan, which he first sang at Bayreuth with Daniel Barenboim in the Harry Kupfer production, which Harry and Sheila attended in the 1990s. On a sweltering day, in a café near the Iron Bridge in Salzburg, over dumplings and bratwurst, Tomlinson describes the characteristics of Harry's music.

JT The first thing that comes to mind is that the vocal score, when it's played [with piano], does not sound anything like the piece when it's played by the orchestra. Here in Salzburg we've had two pianists, both incredibly gifted. One plays the notes as they appear on the vocal score, that is every single note, spot on. The other has spent a lot of time trying to recreate on the piano the sounds one hears from the orchestra. It was my suggestion that they both played at the same time, which might have been the one way to begin to know what Harry's score sounded like, at least on two pianos. They never took me up on that.

But that just demonstrates that this is the sort of music in which you forever hear different things. It's not music which is four beats in the bar. It's long lines of many instruments, in many layers, overlapping each other the whole time. So it's as if you're riding on a sea of sound. At the worst moments it's like being on a rowing boat in the North Atlantic. You basically have no idea where you are. But you're usually more in control than that, if you've learned your part.

It's music like no other. I've done quite a lot of contemporary music, some of it very complex, as well as the Wagner I'm mostly known for. But there's nothing like this. Most new music you learn it very precisely and you sing it very precisely. At any one moment you know exactly where you are. With Harry's music you learn it totally precisely, you sing it in a room totally precisely. You get out on stage and anything can happen. You've got to live by your wits. It's like surfing. You don't know what's going to come next, or what's going to happen. That means you have to prepare even harder. And you've got to ride the waves. It's like a religious experience. You have to give yourself over to it.

Can you pinpoint why it's like that?

JT   Because of the multi-layered, long phrases. The reason you can't put it on to the piano is that it's a percussive instrument. Every note decays almost the moment you strike it. Almost all the notes in Harry's scores are long and sustained. And it's got this incredible sense that it's coming from the bowels of the earth. In the score, for structure, of course it's split into bars – the conductor conducts it as he would anything. But you get the feeling it's only cut into bars to organise it in some way. A lot of it sounds as if there are no bar-lines at all.

     The other thing is the strict formality of everything. In *The Minotaur*, playing that half-man half-beast mythical creature, I have to roar. I began by making a generic bull's roar. But Harry said no, it's got to be a specific sound, a vowel and a consonant, a sound on the word 'Nuarg'. NUARG. It's not attempting to be naturalistic. I think Harry made up the word.

*

The concert that night was given by the Österreichisches Ensemble für Neue Musik conducted by Titus Engel in the resonant, dazzlingly fresh Kollegienkirche, whose baroque excesses have been newly whitewashed over. The acoustic worked ideally for *Verses for Ensembles*, every line and detail of which were clear. Harry's *Bach Measures* and reworkings of Machaut's *Hoquetus David* and Ockeghem's *Ut heremita solus* sounded buoyant and transparent.

    The next night, in a concert given by Klangforum conducted by Sylvain Cambreling, Harry surprised the audience by sitting on the stage in silence while the performers, situated at the rear of the church, invisible but audible on high in the organ loft, performed his *Tombeau in memoriam Igor Stravinsky* (1971).

The idea, suggested by the trumpeter in the über-democratic Klangforum, was that Harry's presence would cue the audience to silence, since the players were out of sight and had no way of showing the work was about to begin. Accordingly Harry walked on stage, took a seat where the conductor would stand, but facing out to the audience, for the duration of the piece – a homage to Stravinsky.

7 August 2013

WILTSHIRE. THE WEATHER HAS BROKEN
AND IS FRESH BUT STILL WARM.
AVERAGE TEMPERATURE 22 DEGREES.

In the garden, the weighty harvest of plums is darkening from green to purple. Most of the early summer flowers are over but several pots of *Gaura lindheimeri* provide a brush of high-summer pinkish-white, bobbing like tiny dancers on the terrace. If the fish are still alive in the pond, they are hiding. Harry has been working long hours since his return, still recovering his energies from Salzburg. We are back at the kitchen table, looking at white clouds.

I had this vision – I suppose it was a dream, a sort of monster dream. I'm sitting on that stage as I did in Salzburg – but I'm looking at myself.

You looked very intense when you were sitting up there . . . it was quite strange.

It was a funny moment. Something I'll remember. I've never done anything like that before.

Did you feel like a magus? You'd conjured up the music from thin air without any evident sign . . . it sounded mysterious, as if from far away. Music of the spheres.

Yes, I'm not sure what I felt. It occurred to me while I was sitting there. I'd written *Tombeau* in response to another composer – I felt I was singing it, my homage to Stravinsky. What are you writing down there . . . ? [*Laughing.*]

You said that Stravinsky indicated to William Glock [BBC Controller of Music 1959–72] that he liked a piece of yours, at which point Glock, who had been fairly ambivalent towards you, became an advocate for your music. Did you meet Stravinsky at that time?

No. There was a regular Saturday concert series in Los Angeles. They did *Monody for Corpus Christi* – my second piece, written after *Refrains* [*and Choruses*].

How did that occur?

It was done by John Carewe in a kind of corridor somewhere in the Festival Hall. They did *Le Marteau sans maître* there – in some sort of space that wasn't designed for concerts. I think the series was called 'Music Now'. So he premiered it with his ensemble, before the Sinfonietta existed.

How did Monody *end up in LA?*

Don't know. But I do know Stravinsky was there. And Glock must have been too. He came back and told me Stravinsky had been positive.

And did you ever get to meet Stravinsky?

I met him very briefly at Dartington, and I met him at Princeton when he conducted one of those late pieces, like the *Canticum sacrum* or something like that. I can't remember. I only met him with other people around.

When did you first meet Boulez?

It must have been when the Sinfonietta did *Verses for Ensembles*. David Atherton did the first performance . . .

Following your L'Etoile lunch!

Yes. But Boulez did that piece a lot, on tour, with the London Sinfonietta. He also conducted *The Triumph of Time* and did it in New York. He made a recording of *Secret Theatre*, *Tragoedia* and some other things – including those Celan songs you heard in Salzburg – at Paul Sacher's place. Recently he did . . . *agm* . . . in Paris . . . So he was quite an ally.

Was your response to Boulez more about his whole musical mind, or his music?

It was his work, really . . .

Is there any common ground in the way you and Boulez compose?

No.

I think more than anything, *Le Marteau* – it's not so much the music or the way he writes music, but there are certain pieces, and I'm just speaking for myself now, that act as a rite of passage. I knew I couldn't be Boulez so I may as well be myself.

I never felt the same about Stockhausen, though he's an emblem of modernism, isn't he?

Did you respond to it? You chose Gruppen *as one of your Desert Island Discs!*

I like everything about Stockhausen except the notes. I just don't like his notes. Does that make sense? I mean, they were wonderful ideas. Another important piece is the early work of Nono – *Il canto sospeso* [1955–6].

Did you know him?

He was at Dartington. Him, Maderna, Berio.

Who was always rude to you . . .

Have I said that? I've said everything, haven't I? But he really was always rude to me, right up until the last. But he was genuinely rude as well.

Not just pretend rude.

No!

Kurtág?

No.
   Have I ever told you my joke about Ligeti?

You mean as in, 'Have you heard the one about Ligeti?' That seems a paradox . . .

Before I had my hut in the garden, I used to work in the front room here where the books are. I had a table there, and a pool table. I was working there one afternoon and the phone went. And a voice said, 'Ligeti here.' And I said, 'That's a surprise' – or something like that, as I barely knew him. And he said, 'I have a problem. I want to live in England but I don't know where.' I said, 'I don't know how to advise you, or even where to start. But I'll do anything to help you.' And he said, 'I have a girlfriend. And she cannot speak Italian, French or German. But she is Japanese and she speaks English.'

That's quite a good joke, I guess.

No. You haven't got to the punchline yet. The punchline is worth a lot of money.

Ligeti went on: 'You know, Harry, we are brothers, you and I.' And I said, 'Well, that's very nice of you. I have a very dear love of your music.' I can't remember what else I said but along those lines. And then I asked him, 'But why do you think we are like brothers?' And he said: 'I have heard that you like custard. And I like custard.' [*Laughing.*]

It's absolutely true. We were brothers because we both liked custard! I don't know where he got that from. I got this picture in my head of the two of us –

Two stony faces of European musical modernism . . .

. . . sitting with big spoons sharing a bowl of custard. So I said, 'Well, if you want to come down here and see where I live, I promise I'll make you some custard.'

And did he?

No.

[Pause.]

He was instrumental in giving me the Grawemeyer Award because he won the first and I won the second. You have to go and be a part of the team if you win it. We didn't choose a winner the year I was on the committee . . . There was some resistance to the fact that all these European composers were winning this enormous American prize.

We haven't discussed where you have got to with the piano concerto.

I've finished the windows. Seven. I think.

And the bits in between?

Well, they're the pictures.

Yes, but have you done them?

Yeah, yeah, all of it.

That's about halfway through?

Yes, more than ten minutes. Forty-five pages.

Did you manage to come back from Salzburg and just carry on? Did having the 'windows' to finish help you?

The windows were predestined. When you have something conceptual, one of the necessary points is the repetition. You have to keep doing it. So I've seen it to the end.

Without being distracted? Or changing your mind?

Yes.

We've talked about it before, haven't we: finding a context for the continuity? Form is manifest. The more you have, there are so many things that are related to the context I've made. The possibilities become less and less. I'm committed. The question of the future – how far I can see ahead – it always seems to be like, if you're walking down the road and there's a person in front of you, that person is the next thing, the thing you're trying to keep up with. Sometimes they move further away, and disappear altogether. Sometimes they get closer, or you get closer, and you're on their heels. When you get to them, it's the back of them. When you see their face, it's never what you think it's going to be, or you think they are.

Do you ever have the feeling of a place you're going to and you invent a place in your head? And when you get there of course it's never what you had in your head. That idea disappears completely and you can't retrieve it. Everything is cancelled out.

I had the experience when I was in Salzburg recently. I had a clear idea of a place, in Salzburg. But I couldn't find at all the place I had in my head. Maybe the place has been completely rebuilt or something –

What, Salzburg? Isn't it more or less untouched?

Well, I don't know. But the place that existed for me, in my mind, has gone.

So in answer to the question 'Do you know where you are going next?' you sort of do and you sort of don't.

I sort of do and I sort of don't. But all I know is the 'windows' had this repeating whatever you wanna call it. The phrase for what goes on in the middle – the custard.

As Ligeti might say . . .

I like the idea that you get glimpses of a music then it's cancelled and something else comes out. But I'm conscious that when I finish this bit it's got to *belong* in some sense. I can't suddenly have a piece of fifteenth-century music or whatever. And what comes after is something completely other. There's a continuum that's being cut up. So there are the seven windows – orchestra tutti – and the last of these windows continues on . . .

Are you on to the slow movement then?

No. I need some solo piano music first. It sort of bursts out . . . and then comes the slow bit.

Oh Christ, I left something in the oven. I forgot I was making a sort of pie. It won't be edible . . .

I leave the house to a smell of burning.

17 August 2013

WILTSHIRE. HIGH SUMMER DOWNPOURS
INTERRUPTED BY SHARP SUNLIGHT.
TEMPERATURE 19 DEGREES.

The plums, now heavy and ripe, are pulling down a bough of the tree. Harry has collected a large bowlful of the dusky purple fruit and is wondering what to cook. Tom Mustill, there to film his godfather, and Tom's girlfriend Amy Cooper assist in the plum harvesting and prop half an old door under the broken branch to support it. Tom has spent the time filming Harry boiling an egg and writing bars of music.

The Moth Requiem *Prom, for twelve female voices, three harps and alto flute, has taken place – the BBC Singers – another event so soon after Japan and Salzburg . . .*

And the same night in Salzburg, Christian Tetzlaff was playing my Violin Concerto . . . which of course I couldn't go to. A man of few words . . .

How did The Moth Requiem *sound in Cadogan Hall? How did it feel compared with hearing the premiere in Holland last October – better, worse, different?*

I didn't think, when I was listening to it, I wrote the piece I wanted to write. But to a degree I feel that with every piece I write. Lost opportunities, ideas I could have developed – hard to say what exactly. You hear things that happened as if by accident, that could have turned out differently. I wrote it under extremely difficult circumstances – Sheila was actually dying during that period. Moths are the metaphor . . .

For life changing, for Sheila, for yourself too, for old age . . .

Yes. Yes. It's about all those. It's about things that are no longer there. I'm nearing the end of my life, at least statistically. But I didn't want to write something indulgent and poetic. Robin Blaser, whose *Moth Poem* I set, had died in 2009. You know about him and the moth?

No.

There was a sound, in a room, every evening. No one knew what it was. Turned out there was a moth in the piano and it had set the strings vibrating in its attempt to escape.

I was feeling sorry for moths. Poor moths. There's a lot of prejudice. Some people see a moth and immediately want to kill it.

People have quite serious phobias about them.

It's the fluttering. And the fact that they're creatures of the night . . . And they eat your cashmere. But in fact there are only two kinds that eat clothes . . .

For what it's worth I enjoyed it more. It's not to do with the quality of the performance. Both were very good.

Aside from the question of mortality and extinction, you have always had a fascination with moths anyway, since childhood.

Yes, I've always thought that if I had more time – one of those things you always think – I'd have found out more about them, but I've never succeeded. I've just read about them as an amateur.

I told you what happened when I was a child?

Not about moths.

[219]

There used to be a thing on children's radio, a natural-history programme. I can't remember what the form was. The entomologist was someone called L. Hugh Newman, an old-style naturalist. He had a butterfly farm in Bexley, Kent. I remember writing to him, aged about twelve, and got a funny typewritten answer.

Then I got a catalogue, and you could buy all the butterfly and moth equipment. I got a butterfly net, and a thing called a relaxant tray which is a tin box with some sort of jelly in the bottom. Once they were killed they would be 'relaxed' and you could set them on a cork board. I did all that. It was mostly moths. There weren't many butterflies around that area of the North at that time.

Not enough flowers?

I don't know. You'd see the usual Cabbage White, Red Admiral, Tortoiseshell. But moths you could get with molasses and beer and paint it on the bark of trees. That attracts them.

Anyway, the cheapest thing – I had no money – to buy in the catalogue were silkworm eggs. Cost nothing. I sent off for them and they arrived. They looked as if they'd been laid on cardboard. You know they're these huge moths – they're called worms but in fact they're moths. I kept them for a while. I put them in a drawer. Nothing happened for ages, God knows how long. And one morning I woke up and the whole wall was covered in these caterpillars, making their way – well I don't know where they thought they were going.

What happened next?

I collected them. You're supposed to feed them mulberry leaves but the sad thing is there were no mulberry leaves in Accrington. But they said you could use dandelions. I managed to get them bigger. They didn't get to the stage of pupae. So they're 'worms' which are really caterpillars. They weave a cocoon around themselves, killing the living caterpillar before it becomes a moth. Then they spin the threads into silk.

Wasn't your mother horrified at all these caterpillars crawling round your room?

No, not really.

And The Moth Requiem?

I used twelve Latin names – and twelve singers split into two six-part choirs, and multi-layered. Robin's poem is interspersed. You can't really hear it as such. You're not meant to. But it's there.

The way the piece comes across is quite particular, with the three harps. The voices have a very specific role, and are used as a kind of incantation. I intentionally avoided melodic invention. I wanted the words to be like declamations. The melodic line comes from the alto flute. There are three distinct layers which are musically separate too. The rhythmic line is dominant.

Why did you use three harps?

They play as a composite instrument. I've written things such as, say, where you would play a unison B, say, and C flat, and then you play it an octave lower and you can have it as a harmonic.

You can mix very dry sounds, harmonics for instance, and percussive sounds which you play with various techniques. But you can also play, simultaneously, notes which are reverberating. There's one technique called 'Xylo'. By stopping the string very near the soundboard with one hand and plucking the same string with the other, it's dead, like a nail. So in one attack you can have 'dry' and 'wet' sounds at the same time.

But *Moth Requiem* will be a piece which is quite hard to programme because of the three harps . . .

In the same Prom there was some truly awful Holst – *Choral Hymns* from the what's it called [*Rig Veda*]? Have you heard them? Terrible stuff. I'm not talking about the singing of course. And then a piece by Imogen Holst which was even worse ['Hallo, my fancy, whither wilt thou go?']. Oof!

But in between they did motets from the [fifteenth-century] *Eton Choirbook* – Walter Lambe and William Cornysh – and they were wonderful. Very rhythmically precise. Absolutely wonderful.

Latin motets – a good complement to the Latin names in The Moth Requiem *as well as being 'your sort of music'. Maybe now you'll write a piece for three harps, given it's your favourite instrument?*

I would quite like to do that . . .

You know I don't feel too well . . . I think I've taken the wrong pills . . .

Let's stop.

23 August 2013

DARTINGTON HALL, DEVON. A WINDLESS, MISTY DAY.
TEMPERATURE 18 DEGREES.

A silvery unvaried sky threatens rain. With the trees – yew, Spanish chestnut, gingko, catalpa – in full leaf, the gardens feel lush and tropical. Harry is sitting on a wall trying to out-stare summer-school enthusiasts who want to take photos or puzzle over his music or explain how now at last, after trying and failing, they are getting the hang of it. He is frustrated at having lost his (expensive, prescription) glasses, the third time in as many weeks. Seasoned composers – Peter Wiegold, John Woolrich (running the summer school) and Philip Cashian – rub shoulders with student composers. The previous night the oboist Melinda Maxwell, pianist Nicolas Hodges and cellist Adrian Brendel gave a concert of Harry's music. The background noise to this short interview is seagulls.

What does it bring back, being here?

It's different this time because usually I have had projects and been very busy. I think I was here for four weeks once. I think the balance has changed over the years, with probably a greater emphasis on amateur music-making than there used to be. When I was here at first, it was in Glock's time – maybe the early 1970s. There was a very serious, solid side with the Amadeus Quartet, the Lindsays, Stravinsky – I didn't meet him then – Hans Keller and so on, Nono, Maderna, Berio, all the Italians. We've talked about this.

Maybe I was a student when I first came. I came with Max and Alan Hacker. I must have come back as a composer, rather than a student, with Nono. I came with the Pierrot Players too, with Max and Alan Hacker.

But you can't condemn the amateurs. The mix has always been part of the ethos.

Yes, I'm not condemning them. I'm just saying that maybe that period of music-making that emanated from Glock was very serious. Then Gavin [Henderson] did it. He had ambition and flair and there was a lot of energy. And John Woolrich has high ideals. But the place has changed and I don't know what's going on and now they've got someone new to run it so I don't know.

See this bird with the white feather [pecking the grass yards away] . . . I've seen it around all week . . .

Do you know him?

Who? The bird?

[Andrew Watts, countertenor, walks past.]

I've just been with him in Salzburg. He was in Gawain . . . *You saw him! And he's here teaching so they have good people.*

[A summer-school participant, a woman of a certain age in shorts, buttonholes Harry and says, 'I did enjoy your piano playing last night . . .']

Piano playing, Harry? No! Not Beethoven Op. 49 no. 2?

No! I did an improvisation with Melinda Maxwell. What happened was that I had an idea. I insisted she was here in Dartington, and Adrian Brendel and Nic Hodges. I said I wanted to do an improvisation. I needed three people to peform. The condition was that they had to be committed to working on it every day. But no one was available at the right time so I did it with Melinda. I made a scheme, very simple, and gave it to her. In no time at all she learned it from memory. So I said OK, what would happen if I played the piano? I think it was rather good. I think they were more interested in the novelty of my doing it . . . playing the piano!

The discussion peters out. Other people come and make passing conversation. Harry fetches coffee from the bar. Melinda Maxwell joins in. The hot, overcast day makes everyone desultory. Suddenly out of nowhere Harry says: 'An Irishman came up to me and said he had just got a grant to study with me. I said I don't take students! He said he could come and stay. I said you can't do that. Anyway he's going to come and see me. We'll see what happens. Maybe he'll make me an offer I can't refuse!'

Toby, Harry's youngest son who is staying all week with his family, comes and sits down, having taken his seven-year-old daughter, Margot, to rehearse for a children's afternoon event, 'Songs in the Garden'. 'Talk to Toby,' Harry instructs, walking off. This conversation takes place on a bench in the gardens with the sound of choral singing in the background: mostly female voices in rich, not always perfect harmony. The American spiritual 'Steal Away' is sung very slowly, several times over.

What was it like growing up with Harry as your father? Did you always know what he was doing? Did you follow his work or speak about it?

TB   I always knew he was a music man, if you like. And I always seemed to think that he must be important in some way because he had people hanging around him. I don't know what it is – he's always held court, like he does. And so, yes, I've always known he was a music man.

But in the sense that you knew he was writing a piece for flute or string quartet?

TB   No. I make no pretence of being interested in what he does.

Except in an objective sense of wanting success for him?

TB   As his son I support what he does. But honestly I am not a contemporary-music person. If he was – I don't know –

a carpenter instead of a music man I still wouldn't have leanings towards contemporary music. I only know it through him. I've never questioned what he does, and we don't actually discuss his music. Or very rarely. (I'm more a Rolling Stones, Ry Cooder or Frank Zappa person, although I know Dad likes a bit of Chuck Berry and Roy Orbison.) There was a record player when we were growing up, but not much choice of albums to play. I seemed to grow up on The Beatles and Simon and Garfunkel . . . I was so keen that when I was seventeen I hitched to London to see the Rolling Stones play. I was gone a week and I should have been at school. When I returned the headmaster calculated the number of hours I'd 'bunked' and I had to sit outside his office studying after school for, I think, four months. (It was well worth it.)

So we have a completely different relationship which has got nothing to do with music.

Do you talk about your own work as an architect?

TB   My work?

I mean what are the shared topics . . . ?

TB   Well, Dad is a teacher. He's always into showing the way and teaching us everything he knows. Cooking. Nature. Not music. Just imparting his knowledge in general. Dad's given me an education which may not be better or worse than anyone else's but it's certainly unique.

[TB] Growing up in a rather nomadic lifestyle, going from the Rocky Mountains – when I was a very young child, around two until six – then Twickenham, then Buffalo, New York, then back to Twickenham then up to Scotland then Paris.

Paris? How old were you then?

TB I was sixteen. I didn't live in Paris. Only visited. They went to Paris when I was still at school. They didn't always take us all with them.

Did you go to many schools?

TB We seemed to. We had to. When they went to Buffalo I was the only one who went. Adam and Silas were – well, I'm not even absolutely sure where they were.

Then they moved to the Lot . . . I don't know how fair it is to say but I always maintain that my parents left home before I did! I was still at school in Scotland when they moved to France. They rang me up one day and said, 'Toby, we're going to move to France. Can you pack up the house? There's a van coming on Saturday morning. We want you to pack the house into the van. It's all going to be taken to France.'

Were you cross?

TB I was very accepting, I suppose. They said they'd sorted out a caravan I could stay in.

Did you live on your own?

TB   Yes, I did as a matter of fact. I went to visit them in France that winter. It was such a bad winter that when I came back the caravan had broken its ropes and rolled down the hill.

And by then how old were you?

TB   Seventeen or so I guess. It had rolled down the hill in the snow. I had to seek shelter elsewhere. I moved with my dog into an abandoned property in the woods with no electricity or water, although I was fed and washed at my friends' house down the track. I had a motorbike to get around on.

Was it terrible?

TB   It was great fun. I tell you, in Scotland I had more freedom than I've had anywhere at any time in my life. I've been trying to recapture that sense of freedom ever since.

Did anyone look after you?

TB   I was young enough for people to have sympathy for me. I had friends . . . Yet I never felt abandoned, I kept Mum and Dad abreast of everything . . . well, most things.

So it's not a sob story?

TB It's absolutely not a sob story. I wouldn't put it across like that. It was a tremendous adventure. I suppose if your upbringing is a bit unconventional, a bit free range, pretty nomadic, and they did kind of leave us to our own devices . . . yet I had a great dependence on them. I didn't know what I was going to do with myself, so when I finished school in Scotland I was a bit lacking in guidance . . . but I enrolled in a foundation course at Chelsea School of Art because that's what my brother had done. It seemed as if art was a good thing to pursue . . .

I think my parents were juggling hot rocks, making it up as they went along . . . Silas was living with the Zinovieffs in Putney. I didn't know where Adam was. For a time my grandparents – my mother's parents – looked after us when my parents were in Pennsylvania.

Yet you got an education of sorts . . .

TB I got an education of sorts! We hung out with amazing people. We were kids interacting with phenomenal people – Morton Feldman for example, Michael Nyman, Hans Werner Henze. I was in my mid-teens, at school on Skye, and Dad said there was this composer coming to stay in our house for a couple of weeks while he and Mum went to Paris.

He said that 'Hans' would cook for us (me and my brother). It turned out it was Henze and his partner Fausto [Moroni]. I was suspicious at first. They stayed with us for two or three weeks and did cook us very good meals indeed (Fausto was the main chef and would return from foraging trips with the most incredible selection of wild mushrooms). When they left it was like saying goodbye to our two new surrogate gay parents: they were very sweet.

Just coming to places like this – Dartington – is an education. We also went on 'holiday' together some ten years ago to Mount Athos in Greece which kind of sums up Dad: he is seriously into medieval architecture and ritual, both of which are in abundance on Mount Athos. We lived like monks for a week, then we went on to stay for a few days with this guy called Paddy in the southern Mani. I didn't appreciate at the time just who this guy was with this most wonderful house overlooking the sea. I am now hooked on reading all Patrick Leigh Fermor's books when on vacation: a true inspiration for me, even in retrospect.

Did you 'do' music as a child?

TB My parents put various instruments in front of me. Cello. I had lessons from Alan Hacker on clarinet. I did a bit of piano. Elgar Howarth gave me a cornet. But I think my parents thought that if there was any obvious musical ability it would have surfaced.

Was it the same with your brothers?

TB Yes, Adam's still got the banjo. I saw it in his studio the other day. I don't think it's ever been played. But Silas plays classical guitar.

[TB]   I used to like going into his hut. Playing on his piano. And he used to have little toys there – I've still got them – that he had when he was a kid: figures, birds, little wild boar, almost mythical, painted and all flaking off. They're in a jar . . .

Did your mother go along with this?

TB   That's interesting. We've all hung out with him but being down here in Dartington you realise everyone's just wanting to see Dad and you get a glimpse of what it must have been like a lot of the time for Mum. There's a lot of hanging around. Everyone just wants to talk about music and you feel a bit out on a limb.

I remember her talking to me about it and saying she'd had to learn to deal with it. She had her own things – watercolours, quilting, all sorts of things like health food and yoga and the Alexander Technique. She was good at finding the positive. When you go to dinner, they all want to talk to Dad or let him talk. And it's not that they're being rude. It's just that's what interests them.

She probably wouldn't have chosen to move around so much, and certainly wouldn't have chosen to move to Scotland.

Dad's a strong man. He's like one of those snow troughs – he clears the way ahead like a snow plough, with Mum the more refined instrument coming up behind and the three children at the rear. If he wasn't such a strong person he wouldn't be able to do what he does.

That's the drive that gets you sawing through rock . . .

TB I can appreciate it, and at the same time there's sometimes been difficulties, inevitably. I know, for example,
I didn't want to move to Scotland. We'd been going up
there in the holidays for a number of years, and there
was this shell of a house right on the beach. But one day
Dad announced – when we were in Twickenham and I
was about twelve – that we were moving to Scotland.

 And I remember being very angry. The idea of being
an English person going to a Scottish island school
seemed like hell to me. But, not necessarily all in
retrospect, I had the best time of my life up there, even
though the weather was shit. We had to board during
the week because we lived on one of the off islands. I
was terrified at first, but as it turned out the others kids
couldn't have been nicer. Those that weren't, I learned
to give as good as I got.

 Soon after Dad was working at IRCAM in Paris
and that's when they went searching in the south of
France . . .

 I really admire him very much. I think it's really
amazing that he has managed to forge this career with
Mum and three kids in tow and all the travelling,
travelling.

*Peter Maxwell Davies – and many other artists – have con-
sidered the life of the artist has to be solitary . . .*

TB He's my godfather.

Did you see him when you were a child?

TB Not really, I was just always aware that I'd been told he was my godfather, but also understood there had been some sort of falling out . . . I still maintained that connection though I didn't see him until last year at the Wigmore Hall. Peter Maxwell Davies and Sandy Goehr and Dad were there and there was this big thing about them being together for the first time in many years.

Dad reintroduced the idea – he took me over to him and said, 'You know Toby, you're his godfather. But you haven't done much for him!' Max took it in good spirit.

Can you see where the drive came from?

TB I think he's very competitive. I think those early days with Max and Sandy . . . I think maybe he had a conviction that he could do it too, as well as any one else – maybe even better.

Where do you think it began?

TB His mother. He's always said his mother was the driving force. Being an only child, you're quite in your head, hanging around that landscape – it's like a combination of all sorts of things, time, place, inclination. All the ingredients.

I don't know whether you've noticed, but Dad's got no family photographs in the house. I noticed there's just a small one of Mum propped up but that's it.

Whereas my wife, Sue's, parents have rows and rows and she'd like the same. I am with Dad by inclination, I don't want to have pictures. But it's not a big issue and I'll go along with her . . .

I'll tell you what's interesting. Dad's basement is below street level and it used to get flooded. He brought up this big box of photographs – or I did – and he was going to throw them away. They were ready for the bin. I saved this huge box of photos, about two thousand of them from the past forty or so years.

Your childhood . . .

TB Yes. A lot of them were damaged, but I separated them out, and unstuck them, and saved what I could. So I've got this bag of photos . . . But Dad was just going to chuck them away.

At the same time, even with all this moving and travelling, Dad has given me a great sense of place. We lived in a log cabin in Colorado. And that wonderful house in Scotland and the fabulous place in France. It's given me a real sense of what home should be. I've lived in lots of interesting places since the caravan: two house-boats, the Barbican, Whitehall! A Georgian house and now a Victorian house in Hackney . . . Dad's not senti-mental. He's not afraid to move on.

By the way, do you know what his schooling was like?

TB I don't know as such. But you can imagine there was probably some sort of Victorian edge to it all. No, he hasn't really talked about that. There are a couple of nice photos hanging around of him in his tank top. He's probably the best person to talk to about it . . . He's probably got some nice anecdotes.

The only one I know is about when you were queuing for your school lunch, like *Oliver!*, there'd be a woman with a big spoon. And she'd try and dollop the mashed potato on to your plate but it would always stick to the spoon and never come off because it was so hard and dry. Then it was a case of knocking it on the side, and you had to catch it when it came off . . .

30 August 2013

WILTSHIRE. A WARM, SULTRY DAY WITH SHARP
SUNLIGHT. TEMPERATURE 20 DEGREES.

The gaura are now a metre high. The garden is still, but for the darting movement of bumblebees and butterflies, comma and tortoiseshell. Harry points out his tomato crop in the greenhouse. 'The colour's nice – yellow – but they don't taste of much.' He is tired, finding it hard to concentrate.

Where are you with the piano concerto?

Lost. Trying to find a logical join. I finished the 'windows' – before I went to Dartington. This week I managed to do some invisible mending. It always comes back to the same thing of knowing what I'm going to do. And I'm never interested when I know what I'm going to do. I have to reinvent the journey. There may be a sort of moment in the piece – whether anyone will notice or just me I don't know – which is like coming out of the thicket.

Have you got over the problem you had when we fixed this meeting the other day?

What was that?

You said you worked late into the night.

Oh yes. I did. Then I threw it all away.

So you worked out the problem and then threw it away?

It's not that simple. I erased the detail and kept the essential thrust of the idea.

Did you sort out the title for the guitar piece?

Well, it is what it is. I had a note from Julian the other day about editing issues that we agreed with Jonathan the guitarist who's playing it, and I've been talking to his very nice lady who does the trust.

We should talk about audiences. It's one thing we haven't discussed but you've often said something along the lines of not caring about the audience, that if they don't like your piece it's their problem. Is that still the case?

We all know what sort of music we have to write to make it pleasing to an audience. I know it seems strange but what I do is all I have. I don't know how to do it any other way. I know the sort of things that have a certain degree of accessibility. If there is a top and bottom of it, a league of understanding, whatever that top and bottom it seems impossible that I can say, OK, I'll address this level or that. I wouldn't know how to do it.

You see I've written a Trio . . . I can identify all of my pieces that are sort of accessible in that sense. People always get very soppy about a piece I wrote – now I can't remember what it is – *The Fields of Sorrow*. Talking to Stephen Kovacevich who was here the other day – he said how much he liked my Trio but I wouldn't know how to do it again. And I couldn't use the things that he was saying . . . I can't accept that there's a model I can use. I *don't do prototypes* . . .

But just to repeat, do you care about the audience?

I don't know how to care. I really don't. What can I do? I'm sweating away trying to make an idea as clear as I can possibly make. Do I have to think about my Auntie Phoebe, what? Oh no, Auntie Phoebe wouldn't like this, should I write a C major chord instead? She'd like that better! What?

*So you're not saying, and have never said, that you don't care
if they hate it?*

No. Only that it's all I can do and I'll try to do it clearly.

Which leads us inevitably to Panic *[1995] and the outburst
against that . . . You've spoken about it before but can you
explain again how it seemed from your perspective? Were you
expecting that reaction?*

No. No, I had no idea whatsoever. First of all it was not
written for the Last Night of the Proms. It was a BBC commission from John Drummond, then director of the Proms.
He didn't say, I want you to write a piece for the Last Night
of the Proms. He put it in of his own accord.

Were you cross when you found it was in the Last Night?

No. I thought it was fun. I think it's the nearest piece I've
got to fun!

Were you shocked?

I was surprised. I was apparently stepping on a tradition, a
sacred cow . . .

You were treading on a sacred cow!

Yes, I was treading on a sacred cow and the attendant
manure. [*Chuckles.*]

Do you get agonised by these sorts of commotions, the fuss . . . ?

No. I don't. The first thing was that I was going to write a piece for John Harle. Now he's a wonderful musician. And you might say that apart from other qualities he has, he's a full-frontal saxophone player. I wanted to write a piece on the side of Dionysus. Instead of Apollo. If you think of what Dionysus stands for, it's a dithyramb. What would you expect? I'm still surprised it had that reaction. When I hear a lot of terrible, cacophonous, so-called popular music . . . My piece has a very strong formal element.

There's more attempt to embrace the audience now . . . especially at the Last Night. The new pieces are usually short and in some way 'fanfares'. Not too taxing, even if good.

Well, I certainly embraced the audience! I'm rather proud of that. And I absolutely wasn't trying. Nothing even entered my head.

But let's come back to this continuum of people – the music-lovers at the bottom of the pile who just like *Swan Lake* or whatever. I actually don't think my music is difficult. Who would be at the top as the most difficult composer? Now who would it be? Say the American – the one who died.

Elliott Carter?

Elliott Carter. The Double Concerto is actually a very obscure piece of music. I actually love it. I'm in front of this situation trying to work out where I'm going to pitch my music . . .

Did you see that thing on the telly about my opera? The thing they do a few nights after?

After what? Which opera, Harry?

When three people talk about it late at night.

The BBC Review Show?

Yes. Something like that. It was after *The Minotaur*. First of all they got someone in who was an authority on music who thought that music anyway had gone completely wrong. Then they had a series of people who knew nothing at all about music who said things like, 'I wanted it to stop.' Unanimously, they disliked it. No one said anything good. There was an Irish poet . . .

Tom Paulin?

Yes, I think so. I could have been from Mars. He was from Earth and he was listening.

Did anyone like it?

No. No one. They got hold of the words 'atonal language' and they really didn't know what they were talking about . . . There you go.

Do you get cross about that kind of thing?

No, but it's a terrible frustration in a way. We seem to have a reaction to music we would never have to painting . . . or any other art form.

Moving on – as you seem to have dried up on this topic – I wanted to ask you about the performers you have written for? Is it chance? Friendships? Is too much made of composers and their interpreters, such as Britten and Pears?

Well, I think the relationship between Britten and Pears was something else because they were married, as it were. I'm certainly not married to the people I write for, and never have been, though of course they've become friends. The standard of performance of modern music is now so high. Whenever I have anything to do with these ensembles that play my music, they're just wonderful. There's nothing I can say. But it wasn't always like that, especially with orchestras.

There's an impersonal side when you work with an orchestra. Very often there's no rapport. They very rarely speak to you. That doesn't mean they're not doing the job, or even enjoying it, but they're professional people. I remember in the early days getting the BBC Symphony Orchestra to do my music was like trying to force water uphill. It's not like that now. I'm often surprised when players do come to me with a part, and ask quite detailed questions.

I remember my worst experience was when the New York Philharmonic did *The Triumph of Time* – they just weren't engaged. It was awful. They weren't interested. As I took my bow, one of the string players said, within earshot – 'Waste of time, not *Triumph of Time*.'

As you were taking your bow? Were you furious?

Well, no . . . It's just how it was.

Do you think your music is hard – to play, rather than to listen to?

Not really. There's plenty that's much more difficult. But I'll tell you one thing about my music: I think it's difficult because there's a lot of it where you have to play together, and that's hard. If it was a lot more contrapuntal, when things are not quite aligned, it would be easier to get away with it! [*Laughs.*] That's why that performance of *Secret Theatre* in Salzburg was so extraordinary: because it was all in the right place. Extraordinary . . .

[By now we are strolling through the gardens of Dartington Hall.]

Have you seen that tree there – in two parts? It looks like two figures kissing. Like two hedgehogs . . .

Sounds like a tale from Ovid. Baucis and Philemon . . .

Maybe it is.

18 September 2013

WILTSHIRE. THE DAY IS A MIX OF GREY AND GOLD.
TEMPERATURE 17 DEGREES. BLUE SKIES WITH BIG
FLUFFY WHITE CLOUDS ARE GRADUALLY EDGED OUT
BY HEAVY RAINCLOUDS WITH SILVER LININGS.
THE SEASON IS ON THE TURN.

Through the window, the garden begins to look tired: gaura and hydrangeas are still in flower and a solitary, late-straggler rose. The evening primrose, no longer covered in moths and bees as they were a fortnight ago, are soldiering on but fading. The ancient, towering beeches – on neighbouring land – are still a rich green but the silver birch has shed its leaves on to the gravel path to Harry's studio. The lawn, too, is scattered with leaves from the plum tree, under which a ladder stands, either for gathering any remaining fruit or to effect surgery on this elderly tree. The figs, which came singly but satisfyingly, are over. The old quince, which Harry claimed to have killed earlier in the summer, remains abundant, if bowed with the weight of its harvest. 'The quinces will be ripe in a few weeks,' says Harry. 'Then I'll bake some . . .'

You've got yet another different kind of tea?

[He is busy unwrapping a foil bag which, like all his other teas purchased in Japan, has an element of lucky dip and gadgetry: he retrieves a flat, scoop-like plastic spoon wrapped in plastic from amidst the tea, to measure the twiggy-looking leaves.]

Yes. I don't know what it is. It's roasted, this one. Smell.

[It smells of musty woods. This aspect of our conversations – the tea ceremony – has been an education, if not entirely a conversion, for this obdurate non-tea-drinker.]

I've just got a new phone. The simplest. The man in the shop asked me what I wanted it to do. I said, well, I don't want it to make porridge. And I'd like it to have one of those dials like old phones used to have where you put your finger in and it goes round. And I want to receive calls, but I don't want to make them. I was stitching him up. He thought he was on *Candid Camera* [a popular TV show in the 1960s involving a hidden camera] though he probably didn't know what that was.

You'd better update me on the piano concerto . . .

My relationship with this piece is very different from usual. I don't know what I'm doing or what it's going to turn out like. I'm being serious. Many more ups and downs. Yesterday I was feeling quite depressed. In the depths of despair, really. Today I am euphoric.

But I wasn't when I got up this morning. Then I went to get some cash out of a hole in the wall and suddenly I saw a way forward. It's as if you are in a room with many locked doors and then you find that one opens and the sun's streaming in. Then the journey ahead looks clear. At least for a bit. It's quite interesting really . . .

We're running out of time for these conversations – only another week or so. You mentioned that you wanted to talk about a few more things before we finish – France, Scotland . . . I still have questions too. Let's start with Scotland. You have quoted from the book you showed me a few weeks ago at the start of your string quartet – The Tree of Strings – which has just been published.

Here's the quote:

> Sir Harrison Birtwistle, the composer – he was my neighbour at Eyre for years. He was a very quiet man: he kept himself to himself. He had three boys – they went away to school in England. Now he's moved to France. He had a beautiful view of the Clarach and the Cuillin from his studio here, but out there, I've heard, he works with his face to the wall and his window looks out onto a planted hedge. He said: 'Having looked on the Cuillin, I know nothing can match them. My going from here is a bereavement – but Raasay is still there in my music, as much as my parents are here in my hand.' And that was it, we haven't seen him since.
> [From Timothy Neat, *When I was Young. Voices from the Lost Communities in Scotland: The Islands*, Birlinn, 2000]

You still look at the wall . . .

Yes. But it's only because it's easier to work that way. Just practical – it's not a determination not to look out on a less beautiful view. Here, I can see down the garden . . . that's lovely. But I still have that sense of bereavement.

Who is speaking in this extract? Who was your neighbour?

He was called Donald. I had two neighbours, probably about a mile away in each direction, and I was in the middle. The Clarach was like the foothills of the Cuillin of Skye, which is a single mountain.

Why did you go to Scotland?

First of all we had the opportunity for one thing – that I can live where I like – though there was a bit of an issue with Toby, wasn't there, when he was at school, but I think he was all right . . .

Toby was cross at the time!

Yes. But I think in retrospect . . . the person who was so much part of all this was Peter Zinovieff. He was such a feature in my life at that time, what with *The Mask of Orpheus* [Zinovieff wrote the libretto], and him being part of the electronic music world, and of Raasay . . .

Zinovieff was one of the reasons for Scotland?

What happened was that he had two houses there. He went there as a young man from Oxford as a geologist – he did his dissertation or whatever on the geology of Raasay. He bought several houses, including mine, which was on the shore in the most beautiful situation. I can't begin to tell you . . . He sold it to me for a thousand pounds. And at that time there was only a ferry, twice a week. So the problem of getting materials and labour to do up the house was enormous. It was virtually impossible. There were many derelict houses.

But then a ferry started, more frequently. I brought all the equipment and material from London, and took builders, and they went up and did it.

Was it a whim?

No, not at all. We used to go there for the summer, every year, to one of Peter's houses. Then this offer of selling the Eyre house came up. I couldn't refuse it. My children had a bit of association with the place. We used to spend all our summers there fishing and sailing and so on. I used to work in a hut on the hillside . . . I know it all sounds idyllic but the weather can be terrible, absolutely awful. It took a lot of energy to do it.

Did anyone else want to move there?

Well, if you waited for anyone to agree you'd never do anything, right? [*Chuckles.*] But I think in all honesty for everyone it was an important experience.

Did you sell Twickenham?

It was rented. Then Silas bought it. But then he moved and bought another house.

Where did you first meet Peter Zinovieff?

He had an electronic music studio, called EMS. Electronic music was very much in the ether at that time. He lived near by in Putney.

Did he approach you or you him?

I approached him. And that started the most extraordinary relationship I've had. It's not easy to talk about him . . .

He was charismatic? With Russian aristocratic origins and a certain eccentric mad-professor glamour?

Yes, he was at that time . . . there was, I suppose, a love-hate element. Extraordinary person. I've said he was a genius without a subject matter. He'd got on to this electronic music thing without any real knowledge of music, though he's a sort of conceptual composer. He relied on composers to articulate his ideas, in a way. He was responsible for inventing some of the most important equipment at the time.

This was pre-IRCAM?

Oh yes. He got friendly with a technical wizard and made this VCF3 – a kind of early synthesiser in a briefcase! A bit like a laptop . . .

[It was designed in 1969 and nicknamed the 'Putney'. Others who used it include Brian Eno, Tangerine Dream, Pink Floyd, Jean-Michel Jarre, Depeche Mode and The Who.]

So you were slightly swept up with his personality, lifestyle and so on?

Yes, I think that's true. It's fair to say that. It was a particular stratum of society in London at that time – the end of the 1960s – rich, champagne-drinking, not quite enough to do, always people around like Laurie Lee, literary types with money, on the edges of art . . .

What appealed to you? What caught your imagination?

Well, the electronic music for one thing. That's how I came to meet him. I'd felt electronic music wasn't going anywhere and I wasn't interested in it. It seemed to me like a parasite, or a tapeworm that ate the music you were writing. Very few people have done anything really interesting. But it led me towards the electronics in *The Mask of Orpheus* . . .

We were always going to work together doing the electronic ingredients but we sort of drifted apart. He had his own problems.

How did the libretto for The Mask of Orpheus *come about?*

We just talked about it . . . it's an extraordinary document. It just happened. They're talking about doing it again, in Holland and here too . . . We'll have to see.

When you lived in Scotland are you saying you were part of an English Bohemian set?

Well, no. Only in that summer period, with the fishing and everything, it might have seemed a bit like that. But once I moved there I kept my own boundaries. I'm glad we went. I wrote a lot of pieces there.

Tell me about the studio again. I think you've referred to it before, but be more precise . . .

It followed on from the studio I had in Twickenham, an octagon which was built for me by students from the AA [Architectural Association]. It was a project for them – a beautiful thing. I had the same concept in Raasay, bigger and with different materials. It was made from blocks and rendered. When I moved to France I did the same again but it had to be in the vernacular, in stone.

How long were you in Scotland?

About seven years. I think we went in 1975 and left in 1982.

Why did you leave?

I was making the electronics for *The Mask of Orpheus* in IRCAM in Paris. That was the *correspondance* – is that what you call it in French, when you change trains? We drove down into south-west France, and made a decision to leave Raasay and live there instead. We looked at two houses and bought the one that had been half done – gutted and completely cleaned up but not finished. It had been decrepit and a speculator had done enough for the new buyer to complete it in the style they wanted. Quite clever really. So once again I was doing a major building project . . .

Did you feel any pressure to move? Or any agony in leaving Scotland, which you'd loved so much?

I think I drew a line. I don't think Sheila wanted to be there any longer. I said if you can sell the house, and we can afford it, we'll do it. And I had an uncle who died who left me a bit of money –

Not Uncle Edgar?

No, my mother's brother, Tom. I'd have liked Edgar. He brought that chest of drawers . . .

Yes, that's where we started these conversations . . . Did you ever feel integrated in France?

Yes and no. We had nice friends and neighbours. We were friendly with a *notaire* and his wife near by . . .

Did you enjoy living in France? You must have felt quite isolated?

I absolutely loved it. It comes back to this thing we were talking about with Accrington and childhood. It was that moment of disillusionment – my parents' house and place – but this seemed to be my ideal, what I wanted from life. I achieved it and got it.

What was it you wanted?

A sort of unfulfilled dream – of weather, nature, everything.

Do you mean this was real, unadulterated? A real Arcady?

Yes. There was still something primitive about it. It was bleak. I loved that.

Why was it bleak? Because there weren't trees? Because the ground was infertile?

All that. Because it was limestone, the *Causses du Quercy* – an arid plateau. Scrub, with a lot of juniper. Then you get the river valleys cut right into it, where it's completely the opposite. Huge gorges. It's one of the really desolate places of France. There were oxen there until 1960. It was in the Lot region.

When I told Boulez I was heading that way he was amazed and said that when he was young no one ever went there – it was regarded as a wilderness, a desert. He said people would travel from Paris to the south to Aix, and down the Rhône to the Mediterranean, or the west to Bordeaux, but that particular place – directly north of Toulouse – was completely neglected. When you look at a map of France you can see it looks very depopulated, though there are big market towns on the way to nowhere – Gramat, Gourdon . . .

You were happy there. Sheila enjoyed it? Why did you leave?

I think maybe Sheila was already getting ill. And she wanted to be nearer the family. I got the teaching thing at King's – I couldn't have done it from there. So it all seemed to fit together, to make a move.

So it's fair to say that came to a natural end too.

Yes. Sure. Then we were in London, by the river, for a bit. Not for long – I like having a relationship to London but not being there all the time. I got terribly depressed trying to find somewhere – I looked all over, in East Anglia too, and found absolutely nothing. This house, now, came about totally by chance. We were having Sunday lunch with Robin [Yapp, renowned wine merchant, whose company is based in Mere]. He said this was available and I could see I could make something out of it. So here again, I found myself almost rebuilding the place. It took eleven months and a lot of money!

I didn't want to come back to this area. I lived here before in the Cranborne Chase years. It seemed like retracing my steps, which didn't seem a good idea for some reason. I thought it would be somewhere I'd like to live though.

And you have?

Yes. Whether it will last I don't know. I have that feeling that I'd like to get rid of everything and live in a different way . . . I don't want it to become like a museum. I don't know how to deal with it. But I love it actually, and to have a place which is ordered. You know I'm terrible with disorder. Have I told you that? My brain won't create order. I have to really

[254]

force myself to put things in the dishwasher. That's why I need this woman to come in every day . . . I don't want to think about it.

As long as I've got a pair of clean underpants.

[Pause.]

You know Henze used to have a huge pile of clean, ironed underpants. I remember thinking, that's what I want to achieve. Seriously. [*Laughing.*]

Did you ever go to Henze's?

No.

He had a villa, built on a labyrinth of Roman wine cellars. It was a house right in the middle of the town with walls and gates. And he lived there with his amanuensis, Fausto, who looked like a Roman god. And a family of peasants. I remember Henze said to me, 'Have you got peasants? How many have you got?'

And I said, 'No, I don't think I've got any.' He said, 'We've got six. No, no! We've got ten!' [*Laughing.*] And they all lived in this place. He lived like a nineteenth-century rich artist, in the grand manner . . .

Did you like his music?

No.

Absolutely not at all?

It doesn't really interest me.

The next day Harry rings me from London to say he has been thinking about the psychological aspects of writing this piano piece. 'It's quite simple, yet quite manic. It's hot and cold. Sometimes I see the way forward, almost every detail of the journey. At the beginning of the week I knew exactly where I was going. But yesterday I couldn't see what I was doing at all. When I'm away I can see it. When I'm close I get stuck and question its validity.' I ask if it is worse with this composition than with any others. 'It's probably always like this. And it's much harder than when, as with opera, there's a narrative. It should be easier but there are endless choices. Have I said this before? Am I making any sense? I want to get back home and get on with it.'

23 September 2013

DRIZZLE. NO WIND. THE AIR FEELS SOFT, MUGGY AND SMELLS OF AUTUMN. TEMPERATURE 17 DEGREES.

The slender gingko – ever visible during our kitchen-table conversations – has tips of yellow in its fan-shaped leaves. The hostas – 'Big Daddy', chortles Harry – are already butter-coloured, the giant, corrugated leaves pockmarked by slugs. A black elderflower still flourishes. The broken plum branch, removed from the old fruit tree a month ago, now rests on a newly dug empty flower bed, allowing its insect inhabitants to carry on their industry. The stepladder in the middle of the lawn leads up to nowhere. The only sound is of water trickling down to the lower level of the rill.

Exceptionally, one short Saturday session aside, Harry has given up his working morning to talk. Again untypically for our conversations, but in line with the time of day, he makes strong coffee, with the same care he applies to his tea-making: new-ground beans, cafetière, warmed milk in a French earthenware jug. He has just returned from a week-end in London. I am about to go to London. Later in the week he is off to Italy. This is therefore the last conversation before this book is due at the publishers in seven days' time. For once he begins the questioning.

So where are you off to with those bags?

London. I'm going to Elektra *tonight at the Royal Opera House.*

Elektra? Lucky you.

Are you being serious? You mean you like Richard Strauss? I thought he was on your list of horrors?

He is. Can't stand him. But I love *Elektra*. Wonderful piece. It's the only one of the operas, mind you. The rest are awful.

Glad we have cleared that up. This is our last session . . .

Oh no!

I wanted to ask, particularly, about the central pillars in your life – two people who perhaps, above all, have enabled you to do what you do with fewest interruptions: your wife, Sheila, and Andrew Rosner, your agent.

Yes – I first met Andrew when he was a young man somewhere in the background at the Sinfonietta. He'd been brave enough to turn away from the family firm – a clothing business I think – and follow his love of music. Nicholas Snowman acted for me for a while and when he went off to Paris Andrew stepped in. It's been a relationship of equals – of private and professional friendship – ever since. He'd come for Christmas, birthdays, to Scotland, to France. The children grew up with him around, he was like a witty uncle with lots of fun and jokes all the time – and that extended to my first publisher, [the late] Bill Colleran at Universal, too, also a constant presence in our lives at that time.

It's quite an extraordinary relationship, isn't it – to have succeeded that long with Andrew, without interruption...?

It's easy to say why: Andrew is totally reliable and responsible in every way. He's loyal and never makes a fuss and has dedicated himself to the task for forty years.

You've mentioned Sheila many times, but we haven't discussed where you met?

We first met in that in-between period before I became a student. I was taking lessons at the Northern School of

Music and so was she. Then we didn't meet again until after I left the Army in 1956 or 1957. By then I was at the Royal Academy of Music. I saw her one day in Baker Street, crossing the road with her mother. We got married soon after.

It seems that your working life and stability would have been impossible without her.

Absolutely. She was a mainstay. It's simple really: with an extraordinary tolerance, she let me get on with it. I'm sure it wasn't always easy. The long years of her illness were difficult, and in an immediate sense a relief when they were over. But life is different now. Trying to settle down into new routines, with a different focus which is gradually shaping into a new life. I haven't had experience of this aloneness before . . .

We have a few loose ends to tie up before we finish . . .

Actually I was thinking of something Pissarro said. When I got back last night I dug out this catalogue [*out ready on the kitchen table*].

Read these two quotes: first Pissarro, then Cézanne:

'In all the schools, one is taught to do something in art: this is a vast mistake; one merely learns to execute, but truly never to create art: never! [. . .] I started to understand my sensations, to know what I wanted, when I was in my forties, but only vaguely; when I was fifty, that is, in 1880, I had an inkling of the idea of unity, but I could not express it; at sixty, I am starting to see a way of expressing [it]. Well, do you really think that one can be taught all this?'

Here is how Cézanne explained Pissarro:

'We may all descend from Pissarro, he was lucky enough to be born in the West Indies, there he learned drawing without masters.'

So this sums up how you see yourself? The not being taught and having to find your own way through?

Well, yes, I think it does really.

And the stuff about really getting going in his forties?

That too.

They are especially pertinent because there is only one thing we still haven't talked about.

Oh yeah?

You know what it is.

No.

Harry, it's the subject you have refused to talk about all through this book.

Oh really?

But you know we can't finish without addressing it.

Oh. Oh. Uh.

You agreed you'd tell me . . .

Tell you what?

About school. Harry, we can't finish this book without talking about it in some way . . .

[*Small-voiced*] You can.

We can't.

[*Child-like, more desperate*] You can.
   I thought we'd got away with it.

Got away with it?

I thought we had, you see.
   I thought we'd swept it under the carpet.

We haven't swept it under the carpet. We're going to try to talk about it now.

[This exchange continues for several minutes. By now I feel – very uncomfortably – like a primary-school teacher trying to retrieve plasticine from a child's fist, variously cajoling and stipulating. Harry is not remotely cross, but he is immovable.]

You promised. I can't, wouldn't, force you. But we can't leave the subject – it's a cliffhanger . . . we have to address it.

I could talk about it. Maybe. One day. But not for a book.

Well, this is for a book . . . !

So.

[Long pause.]

In that case we have to find a way of not talking about it.

OK. That's the interesting thing.

So if I ask you questions, will you answer them in your own way, even if the answer is 'no comment'?

All right. I'll see.

What was it like?

You have to believe me. I don't want to say.

What can you tell me that could go into a book – a book that has been skirting round the subject since the first pages . . .

Yes. I want to go on skirting round it. I've been skirting round it all my life. I want to skirt around it now.

OK. Without telling me what you are skirting around, can you tell me why you are skirting?

Well, that's telling you. How can I not tell you about it while telling you . . . or tell you while not telling you . . . ?

Did you actually go to school? Did you skip school?

[Silence.]

Is there anything else you want to talk about? That's missing?

Not really, Harry.

Can it not be talked about as an issue I refuse to talk about?

So far all our conversations have been dialogue rather than interrogation. This is the only wall we have come up against . . .

Yeah. I know.
    But isn't it as interesting that I refuse to talk about it . . . ?

Of course it's interesting! But I'm not sure how to move forward. Was it painful, school, can you answer without betraying yourself . . . ?

No. Well, in retrospect – no, here we go.
    It has been painful avoiding the whole business in the intervening years. At the time, as a child, you accept the

status quo. You don't simply come to a conclusion about the situation. It's just what you are doing at that moment.

So you mean you have studiously enclosed it, encircled it, in adult life, as something you avoid?

Yeah. And it was the whole thing of being a musician, as an instrumentalist, that gave me a way to retain this inner thing . . . It gave me the way . . .

All along, though, I never knew that I would be able to do anything with this 'other' thing, it was something overriding which I always hoped was something that would develop.

I can see that at that period of schooling, the 1940s and early 1950s – and, again, I am not asking you to talk about anything you don't wish to – but in that era notions of dyslexia, which you have spoken of as being a burden to you, were non-existent . . . There were the clever people who could read and spell and the others who couldn't, who were thick . . .

That's right. The so-called intelligent ones were weeded out and given a different education. The rest . . .

You felt that was you?

Yeah. But the other side to me, this 'otherness', gave me a sort of confidence which manifested itself as a kind of arrogance which I have managed to resolve. I think I'm quite a nice person really. [*Chuckling.*]

[264]

But I imagine that happened later, maybe in your twenties when you were able to do your own thing and you weren't being measured by school standards?

Yes, that's right. But part of the arrogance was also the idea of the artist, the tweed suits, Dylan Thomas, you know . . . the kit that went along with it.

But being in a college of music, that side of it – the look – was a defence mechanism in a way. To dress up now is part of life. You see people everywhere in funny clothes, things up their nose, what? But the external manifestation then . . . I think people were called Bohemians.

Consequently from my upbringing and schooling I was much less developed, in every way, than Max and Sandy. Than everyone really!

While you in one sense had that inner confidence, did you also feel you had to recover from a bruising experience at school? Or was it not as clearly defined or as uncomfortable as that?

I think the sense that I was taken seriously, after school – when I became a student . . . that all helped . . . I don't know.

We talked before about how you got to Manchester . . . Which in effect you did mostly by yourself, the scholarship and so on . . .

Yes. Pretty much on my own. I think that if I hadn't had this 'other' side I'd have ended up as an accomplished second clarinet in the Hallé Orchestra or something.

Your mother would have been pleased.

Everyone would have been pleased. It's a fine thing to be.

But you've got to remember that before I became an official music student I'd done an awful lot of stuff in writing music – on my own, not knowing much history or theory of music, not knowing the difference between Hindemith and Schoenberg – if you like. They're quite good examples. They were just names.

At the Hallé in Manchester John Barbirolli played Mahler and he played Vaughan Williams. I don't know what I was emulating in my own music. All I was really emulating was being a composer. I don't know how it fitted stylistically into anything.

[An industrial tool outside in the street, perhaps a saw, repeatedly makes the sort of sound too often associated with contemporary music: a chromatic, nasal slide between E and C. It is sufficiently distracting to interrupt Harry's train of thought.]

Another straight question –

Yeah. Go on.

We've talked about you being an only child and finding your way – but this school thing, did you feel totally isolated? Were you the boy who –

The boy who sat in the corner on his own? No. Absolutely not. I had chums. But then I probably joined in with them as some aspect of me was a tearaway . . . I remember doing terrible things . . .

Such as?

No. No! [*Chuckling*] We're not going there.

We all did terrible things . . .

But you see because of where I came from, the social thing – and historically, it being through the war and straight after – I mean the sort of kids I went to school with meant I witnessed extreme poverty. There were people who didn't have proper clothes to wear.

Socially I was slightly to the side of all that because firstly I made music, and secondly I was a farmer's boy. I was different from the children whose parents worked at the mill, or at the iron foundry, or making bricks, which I think most of them did.

So even if you didn't articulate that, it must have given you a sense of slight superiority . . . or a sense of self?

I don't think it was superiority. Or maybe it was.

You knew you had the possibility of a different kind of life?

Certainly I did.

So probably – I'm guessing – the things you want to keep

[267]

closed away, out of reach, were probably not that sensational, and if you prised the lid open you – we – might even be disappointed?

Yes. Certainly.

Any deed or event at school you might reveal just couldn't match up in sensational value to the importance it had in your life?

Exactly. I think that's true. It only meant something to me. And that's still true.

You might say you stole sweets or flattened car tyres or threw stones through windows, but it probably wouldn't be much worse than that?

No.

So it would waste it to tell it. Sort of pouring it down the drain . . .

Yes. It means more to me than could be shared in the telling.

It's part of the landscape of your childhood.

It's that exactly. The landscape . . .

[He retrieves his laptop – with which he is now considerably more proficient than he was a few months ago – and finds recent images of the surviving shell of Huncoat Power Station, derelict, half dismantled, mossy, covered in graffiti.]

This is what they built.

So what are we looking at exactly?

It's just part of the power station – they just left it like this when it fell into disuse. Truncated. All overgrown. Abandoned.

We were trying to remember the Tarkovsky film . . .

Stalker. This is *Stalker.* Look at this . . . This was my father's land.

Your father's land? You mean it was right on his land? So close to you?

Yes. This is what they built up to my father's land on the boundary, at the back of my house. I was twelve or thirteen.

Your Arcady . . . ravaged. Did you ever go inside when you were a child?

No, because it was in use. But I went up the cooling towers. In the distance, across the fields, you can see Pendle Hill. You could see it from my house.

[Pendle Hill was associated with witchcraft – the Pendle Witches – and with the early Quakers. George Fox (1624–1691) had a vision at the top of this isolated plateau of which he wrote in his Autobiography: 'As we travelled, we came near a very great hill, called Pendle Hill, and I was moved of the Lord to go up to the top of it; which I did with difficulty, it was so very steep and high. When I was come to the top, I saw the sea bordering upon Lancashire. From the top of this hill the Lord let me see in what places he had a great people to be gathered.']

Childers Green was my house. That was the name of it. Now it's a cattery. I've told you this.

[He searches images on the Internet and looks through them, silently.]

But this, all this [woodland, scrubby fields] is adjacent to this terrible thing you've just been looking at.
    Anyway I . . . [*Falls silent, melancholy.*]

You've often talked of being disillusioned about that place . . . Was it specifically the power station going up? Or was it the fact that you realised that what had been your childhood paradise was in truth so tiny, crowded in by industry, mining, mills . . .

Well, it was – yes, yes, it was tiny . . .
    But we've done all this, haven't we?

Yes, we've done all this. Do you feel we have still managed to sweep 'it' all under the carpet, as you wanted.

It's up to you.

I mean I hope you don't feel too exposed?

I don't know.

I think what you have said this morning is entirely consistent with what you have said, or alluded to, throughout our conversations . . .

[Silence. For several minutes he continues searching Google images of Childers Green.]

You can see my house. Here [*points to white dot*]. It's too small to see properly. Pebbledash. Very low building.

I know your ongoing anxieties, your neuroses, as you describe them, which are part of what enable you to do what you do . . .

Enable me? Do you mean as if it's a sort of illness . . . ?

No. I'm trying to formulate a thought . . .

We're all like that, aren't we? Does it make me different from anyone else?

No, it doesn't. But we are talking about you and how it shapes your work. You hold dear to you something – as we all do in different ways – very raw and precious and private in you

[271]

about that little boy, growing up in that scrap of desecrated landscape, finding your way to new horizons . . .

Yes. I do. Absolutely. But does that make me any different?

No. I'm trying to say that as we reach the end of these conversations, the seasons have turned – spring into summer, and now autumn closing in . . . a cycle which repeats and whose rhythms have always been part of your life and your music. Think of the music of the changing seasons in Gawain . . .

Yes.

So my question is what sort of continuity – to use your word – is there between being that child, with that strange, as yet untested belief, and who you are now?

One thing is that in a sense I've achieved much more than I ever imagined. But then again I didn't even dream of . . . I've never felt I had ambitions for myself, only for my idea, and for it materialising into something worthwhile. [*Laughing*] But I'm still here, still trying. And I'm still exactly the same.

Of course. And what none of us can ever know is the point at which we feel we've 'got there'. When you're in your twenties you think it'll all be clear by your forties but then really it never is . . .

The thing that gives me confidence is that it's somehow happened at all. If I stop to look back I think – well, they've actually performed that piece in the Salzburg Festival . . .

But also, it's still challenging you.

It's still challenging me.

You still don't know what you're doing – in a sense! Or that's what you have said so many times . . .

And it's true. A very good example is this piece I'm writing now, the piano piece.

And how is it going?

Not well. Not well at all.

Would you ever say it was going well?

I feel I'm up against time and one thing and another.

Are you into your 'slow movement' yet?

No. Maybe I never will be. It's always the next bit . . .
   [*Laughing*] It'll be all right though.

Although you're not very self-regarding – I don't imagine you counting the number of operas or orchestral pieces you've written . . .

Absolutely not.

. . . perhaps there's a sense in which, as that child in a small,

rural oasis, you planted a tree . . . and not to push the metaphor,
it's struggled up through hard ground and spread branches.

I give you permission to use that metaphor.

There's that elusive sense that you're being given permission, encouragement, to have another go, to see if this time you can make whatever it is work. I've just had a sleepless night, last night. I thought this morning, I can see a way forward. But I can guarantee that this afternoon, when I sit down, I won't be doing what I thought at all. As usual.

[Pause.]

I think I've had ambitious ideas. I would never have written *The Mask of Orpheus* or *Gawain* without pretty ambitious ideas?

That's why I think that thing – the Pissarro text – I mentioned earlier, it always struck me as being important. I wish I could have said that, or articulated it in that way.

You have talked about various pieces – Carmen arcadiae *for example – which seem to be the most precious to you?*

That's true.

Can you tell me which? Am I asking what you'd call a 'music-lover's question'? I'm trying to reach something less obvious than that . . . a sense of how you feel you have best represented yourself.

Whatever you do, you take something and push it as far as you can. It becomes focused, completely, like looking at

[274]

it through a microscope, the essential thing, the core. I'm always wary of making comparisons but I think that's what happens in *The Art of Fugue*. Or the *Musical Offering*. Where Bach took the notion, the essence – the '48' Preludes and Fugues, one in every key – or Messiaen did that 'Mode of Values' [*Mode de valeurs et d'intensités*, 1949], where he gave every note a value, and every note a dynamic. That was a huge influence on modern music, particularly Boulez.

One thing we haven't talked much about – you used to use those lists of random numbers as an aid, but you no longer do.

It's difficult to talk about because it gives a wrong impression, as if it's the knit-one-pearl-one method of composition. Or Harry's Housey-Housey version of composition!

But it's a technical thing we didn't address.

I don't need it now. I can fake it! Well, fake it is the wrong word. But I've worked out how to do what I need. Random quality – supposing you have ten increments and I said put them in any order you want, I guarantee that putting them through an order based simply on intuition would be very different from putting them through a real random process. It does something intuition never could.

What it did for me was give me a distance from it. It means you have to accept certain rules and then you can reject them. But it's not a big deal.

[He starts scrubbing jam off the table. It's hardened to a sticky skin. Then the phone rings, first Jochen Voigt, then Adrian Brendel. Then the street machine repeats its C-to-E sawing noise. Random numbers have had their moment.]

We can stop soon.

Really? Already?

I've got to catch my train. To ask again – the pieces that mean most?

It's not total pieces as much as moments and details. They are there to a lesser or greater degree in things. I learned something – this quality is something I was striving for and sometimes achieved. In one way I want to be completely in control.

Which you never can be?

Which you never can be.

So specifically?

Well, *Tragoedia* [1965]. The piece I wrote first – or the first where I felt was doing what I wanted to do. I'd rejected what I thought were Boulez forgeries.

You were thirty-one.

I'd written a piece called *Monody for Corpus Christi* [1959]. I thought I'd made an imitation of Boulez though I can see now that's not what it was . . . Whatever I thought, something else happened in *Tragoedia*. Because I felt that all the things I'd been going on about, since the age of twelve, thirteen, fifteen – and which I left off when I became a music student – somehow I'd picked up the threads again, but in the light of being a music student and all that I'd gained. Not necessarily proficiency but other experiences. With *Tragoedia* I felt I'd found a way back.

And more recently?

I think *Secret Theatre* is pretty good, for me. Were you there for that performance [in Salzburg]?

Yes. We've discussed it at some length!

That was pretty good, wasn't it?

Yes.

And were you there when I sat in front of the audience? [*Laughing*] That was pretty funny.

Yes, I was there.

[*Still laughing*] Is that going to be in the book?

Yes.

But the other thing in terms of achievement, I've also taught at Harvard! I have a professorship at King's! That's quite funny really.

It's a sort of boo sucks to the education system really.

[Pause.]

How are your quinces?

They're still there. They're not ready. Why, do you want some?

It was just an enquiry . . .

They'll be ready when the smell comes in through the kitchen window. I read that somewhere. I think it was Jane Grigson.

It won't come in through this kitchen window here.

No, too far away. I think they're quite late. I've seen them there when the leaves have gone.

That could be soon.

But you have to smell them to know if they're ripe. And when they are I'll wrap them in foil and bake them or turn them into jam.

11 *October 2013*

WILTSHIRE. BRIGHT. LOW SUN AND CLOUD. COOL
BREEZE, AUTUMNAL. TEMPERATURE 13 DEGREES.

Harry has been working at the kitchen table with David Harsent. After breakfast they swap childhood memories, joining together in singing 'Jesus Bids Us Shine' and a rude version of another hymn – both from the *Baptist Hymnal*, part of their shared history. The first draft of this book having been sent to the publisher already, I have returned to go through corrections.

David departs and the Polish cleaner, with her two over-active mobile phones which ding and chime in not quite C major every few minutes, arrives. We move out of her way into the sitting room, serene, light-filled, minimally decorated, with a glass extension looking onto the garden and windows on three sides.

One side of the lawn is plunged into darkness. The other, as if divided by a ruler, is bright and filled with dazzling October sun. The earth is damp. The black leaves of the elder have fallen. The remaining quinces – most have been harvested and placed in Harry's Afghan bowls in the kitchen ready to be made into jam – hang high on the tree, catching the sharp light like golden fruit in a nursery-book illustration. The young gingko has turned into a column of saffron yellow, a totem of one season ending, another beginning.

Harry has said on an earlier occasion that he isn't sure how to use this room. Sheila often sat there in her final years. The colours are neutral, natural. Several spherical shapes –

a round floor lamp, a globular footstool, small 'crystal' balls carefully positioned in a blue glass bowl – create a sense of geometry, offsetting the straight lines of a pair of sofas and some big, abstract pictures. A shelf of terracotta pots adds to the order and stillness. All that moves is the light, reflecting and refracting on the ceiling like a ghostly kaleidoscope. Harry switches on the hi-fi.

Listen to this. More of my melancholy music . . .

[The CD is of *Pièces de Viole du Second Livre* 1701 by Marin Marais, played by Jordi Savall. In the short opening Prélude of the Suite in E Minor, theorbos and viols wrench, pull and strain against one another in unending dissonance, almost a torment to hear.]

I don't know why I love this, but I do . . . Now listen to this. William Lawes. [*Consorts to the Organ*, played by Phantasm on a Linn Records CD.] Do you know Laurence Dreyfus?

He writes about Bach? . . . We talked about him a while ago when you were listening to this same disc before . . .

He's playing treble viol here. I love him. He doesn't know it but I do!

You know Lawes was born around here? Salisbury, I think. I want to make – what do you call it – a paraphrase of Track 9, the Paven from the Set a5 in C minor, for Melinda Maxwell [oboe], Adrian Brendel [cello] and a harpist.

[We listen to the Paven. Halfway through he asks me to swap sofas and look into the blue bowl where the small glass balls are interacting with the low, blinding sun. Harry sits directly opposite. By a quirk of light, a series of reflections mirrored by their refracted selves, his face appears in strange, multiple image in the bowl and the glass ball, as the clouds move and obscure the image. It's a union of physics and magic – and just the kind of quixotic moment Harry loves.]

[*Asked in pantomime fashion*] Can you see me? Take a photo.

[I try, none too successfully, to capture this moment on my smartphone.]

I've thought of a title for the piano piece. It was going to be '*Correspondance*' but then I realised people would call it 'Correspondence', or 'Correspondent' or 'Correspond'.
So I think *Responses* will do.

As in the liturgical questions and answers?

Yes. Because they don't echo each other – the orchestra doesn't necessarily say the same thing. And the piano generates a list of unanswered questions.

The title may be too close to Boulez's Répons?

Yes, I realised that . . . I may have to go on thinking.

Let me know when you decide . . .

Did I tell you what a strange piece it is? It really is. Some days I don't want to go on and others I feel euphoric.

And that isn't how you usually feel?

No, never.
Are you going to go now?

Yes, soon. One other thing I wanted to check – it's something Adam said about school, but you may not want to talk about it – and it's fine if you don't. He said you removed a brick each day so that the school would disappear . . .

That's not quite what happened. We were the big boys at the gate, saying we'd biff the younger boys if they didn't bring a material piece of the school out with them – a brick or some other piece of the fabric . . . Later I was beaten for it.

And the school didn't vanish despite your efforts?

No, unfortunately.

Thank you for telling me that.

Do you want some quinces? Or some of these apples? They're wonderful. Next time the jam will be ready.

I'm off now, Harry.

OK.

[He gestures towards the garden in the direction of his studio.]

And I'm off too, to do a bit more knitting . . .

HARRISON BIRTWISTLE TIMELINE

1934 Born 15 July in Accrington, England.

1941 His mother buys him a clarinet and he has lessons with the leader of the Accrington military band, which he eventually joins.

1945 Begins composing. Few early works survive, with exception of *Oockooing Bird* for piano (*c.* 1950).

1952 Wins scholarship as clarinettist to Royal Manchester College of Music (now the Royal Northern College of Music), where he studies with Frederick Thurston (clarinet) and Richard Hall (composition). Fellow students include the composers Alexander Goehr and Peter Maxwell Davies, the trumpeter Elgar Howarth and the pianist John Ogdon.

1953 With fellow Manchester students founds the New Music Manchester group as a vehicle for exploring important twentieth-century works as well as for playing their own music.

1954 Hears Messiaen's *Turangalîla-symphonie* in London, conducted by Walter Goehr – 'an absolute magical moment'.

1955 Undertakes National Service (1955–57) as a clarinettist with the band of the Royal Artillery.

1956 Only London concert by New Music Manchester group (9 January), organised by William Glock at the Institute of Contemporary Arts, including works by Goehr, Maxwell Davies, Lutyens and Hall, but not Birtwistle, who appears only as clarinettist.

1957 Attends a London concert (6 May) where he first hears Boulez's *Le Marteau sans maître* – a formative experience. Undertakes postgraduate clarinet studies (1957–58) with Reginald Kell at Royal Academy of Music, London, followed by a short period playing with Royal Liverpool Philharmonic Orchestra. Completes his 'Opus 1', *Refrains and Choruses*, on New Year's Eve.

1958 Signed up to be published by Universal Edition, with whom he remains until 1994. Marries Sheila Duff. Undertakes variety of non-musical jobs.

1959 *Refrains and Choruses* selected by Society for the Promotion of New Music and premiered at the Cheltenham Festival by the Portia Wind Ensemble. Birth of first son, Adam.

1960 *Three Sonatas for Nine Instruments* chosen by SPNM for performance at Aldeburgh Festival, but withdrawn after first rehearsal. Score unpublished, but now housed at Paul Sacher Stiftung, Basel, Switzerland. John Ogdon premieres *Précis* for solo piano at Dartington Summer School. During this period teaches at three Dorset preparatory schools: Claysemore School and Knighton House (Blandford), and Port Regis (Shaftesbury).

1961 *Monody for Corpus Christi* selected to represent Britain at ISCM Festival.

1962 Appointed Director of Music at Cranborne Chase Girls' School, Wardour Castle, Dorset (1962–65).

1963 Pupils of Knighton House and Port Regis Schools

give premiere of *Music for Sleep*, commissioned by *Musical Times* and *Music in Education*. His second son, Silas, is born.

1964 Co-founds (with Goehr and Maxwell Davies) the Wardour Castle Summer School, with Michael Tippett as President. *Entr'actes and Sappho Fragments* premiered at Cheltenham Festival.

1965 *Tragoedia* premiered at second (and last) Wardour Castle Summer School to great critical acclaim. His third son, Toby, is born.
Wins a Harkness Fellowship for two years' study in the USA. Becomes Visiting Fellow at Princeton University, where he completes the composition of *Punch and Judy*.

1967 Completes his American studies at University of Colorado at Boulder. Co-founds Pierrot Players with Maxwell Davies and Stephen Pruslin. Their first concert at Queen Elizabeth Hall, London, includes premiere of *Monodrama* (later withdrawn) to a libretto by Pruslin and dedicated to Maxwell Davies.

1968 *Punch and Judy*, to a libretto by Pruslin, premiered at the Aldeburgh Festival in the presence of Benjamin Britten. *Nomos* commissioned by the BBC Proms and premiered by Colin Davis and the BBC Symphony Orchestra. Approached by newly established London Weekend Television to write a TV opera on the subject of Orpheus, but project falls through.

1969 *Down by the Greenwood Side*, to a text by Michael Nyman, premiered at the Brighton Festival. Peter

Zinovieff collaborates for first time on tape parts for *Linoi*, *Four Interludes for a Tragedy* and *Medusa*. Approached by Royal Opera House Covent Garden to compose an opera that eventually becomes *The Mask of Orpheus*, to a text by Zinovieff. Commission later passes to Glyndebourne (1973), then English National Opera (1975).

1970 Premiere in London of *Nenia: The Death of Orpheus*, to a text by Zinovieff. The Pierrot Players disband (and become the Fires of London).

1971 *An Imaginary Landscape*, a BBC commission, is premiered by Pierre Boulez and BBC Symphony Orchestra at ISCM Festival in London.

1972 *The Triumph of Time* premiered in London by Lawrence Foster and Royal Philharmonic Orchestra. Writes his only film score to Sydney Lumet's *The Offence*, with electronic realisation by Zinovieff.

1973 Appointed Cornell Visiting Professor of Music at Swarthmore College, Pennsylvania. Begins composition of *The Mask of Orpheus*, Acts 1 and 2 (1973–75). *Chronometer*, his only piece exclusively for tape, prepared with Zinovieff, is premiered in London.

1974 At invitation of Morton Feldman appointed Visiting Slee Professor at State University of New York at Buffalo (1974–75).

1975 On return from America moves to island of Raasay in Inner Hebrides. Appointed Music Director, National Theatre, London. Scores include *Hamlet* (1975), *Tamburlaine* (1976) and *Volpone* (1977).

Also works on other productions in collaboration with composer Dominic Muldowney, including *Julius Caesar* (1977), *The Cherry Orchard* (1978) and *As You Like It* (1979).

1977 *Bow Down*, to a text by the poet Tony Harrison, is premiered at National Theatre.

1981 Writes highly acclaimed music for Peter Hall's production of Aeschylus' *Oresteia* trilogy at National Theatre in a new translation by Tony Harrison. Featured composer at Huddersfield Contemporary Music Festival. Resumes composition of *The Mask of Orpheus*, Acts 2 and 3 (1981–84).

1982 Becomes Associate Director, National Theatre, and moves to Lunegarde in the Lot region of France. Begins work at IRCAM, Paris, with composer Barry Anderson, on the electronic music components for *The Mask of Orpheus*.

1984 London Sinfonietta premieres *Secret Theatre* at his fiftieth-birthday concert at the Queen Elizabeth Hall. Invited to Japan for a major retrospective of his music in Tokyo. First full-length study of his music published by Michael Hall (*Harrison Birtwistle*, Robson Books, London).

1985 Directs Summerscope Festival at London's Southbank Centre under the title 'Harrison Birtwistle: His Fancies, His Toys, His Dreams'.

1986 Premiere of *The Mask of Orpheus* by English National Opera at London Coliseum, conducted by Elgar Howarth and Paul Daniel, directed by David Freeman. Wins prestigious Grawemeyer Award from the University of Louisville. *Yan Tan Tethera* premiered by Opera Factory/London Sinfonietta at Queen Elizabeth Hall. *Earth Dances*, another BBC commission, is premiered by the BBC Symphony Orchestra, conducted by Peter Eötvös – 'a desolate, disturbing rite of spring for this decade' (Nicholas Kenyon). Made Chevalier des arts et des lettres by French government and Honorary Fellow of Royal Academy of Music.

1987 *The Mask of Orpheus* wins the Evening Standard Award for Opera. *Endless Parade* is premiered by trumpeter Håkan Hardenberger and the Collegium Musicum of Zurich. The work is commissioned and conducted by Paul Sacher and this association leads in 1989 to the Paul Sacher Stiftung's acquisition of all the manuscript material in Birtwistle's possession and an ongoing archival relationship.

1988 Knighted by Queen Elizabeth II. Major BBC Birtwistle festival ('Endless Parade') at the Barbican Centre, London including UK premiere of his trumpet concerto *Endless Parade*.

1989 Discovers poetry of Paul Celan in translation and begins *9 Settings of Celan* (1989–96).

1991 *Gawain* premiered at the Royal Opera House Covent Garden. Wins Evening Standard Award for Opera a second time. Featured composer at Wien Modern festival.

1992 *Antiphonies* premiered in Paris by Philharmonia Orchestra and Joanna MacGregor (piano), conducted by Boulez. Appointed to Board of the

Southbank Centre, London (1992–2002).

1993 Appointed Composer-in-Residence to London
Philharmonic Orchestra.

1994 Appointed first Henry Purcell Professor of
Composition at King's College, London (1994–
2002). *Gawain* revived at the Royal Opera House in
revised version, followed by a recording (Collins
Classics 1996). *The Second Mrs Kong* premiered
by Glyndebourne Touring Opera and subsequently
revived at Glyndebourne Festival (1995), with
further new productions (in German) in Heidelberg
and Vienna. Tour of *Earth Dances* by Cleveland
Orchestra conducted by Christoph von Dohnányi
includes USA, Salzburg Festival and the BBC Proms,
followed by a recording (Decca 1996).

1995 Awarded the Ernst von Siemens Foundation Prize.
Tribute concert of *Secret Theatre* and *Endless Parade*
given in Munich. Moves to Boosey & Hawkes Music
Publishers. *Panic* premiered at the Last Night of the
Proms to controversial critical acclaim.

1996 Moves from France to new permanent home in Mere,
Wiltshire. *Pulse Shadows* premiered in Witten,
Germany. Southbank Centre's 'Secret Theatres'
Festival includes UK premiere of *Pulse Shadows*
and a new semi-staged production of *The Mask of
Orpheus*, followed by a recording (NMC 1997).
Mitsuko Uchida is soloist in US premiere of *Anti-
phonies* with Los Angeles Philharmonic and Boulez.

1997 Appointed Director of Composition at Royal
Academy of Music, London.

1998 *Exody* premiered in Chicago by the Chicago Symphony Orchestra, conducted by Daniel Barenboim, followed by its European premiere at the BBC Proms. Simon Rattle conducts *The Triumph of Time* with City of Birmingham Symphony Orchestra in UK and at Konzerthaus in Vienna. Made Fellow of King's College, London. Update to Michael Hall's study of his music published (*Harrison Birtwistle in Recent Years*, Robson Books).

1999 Rattle conducts *Earth Dances* with CBSO in UK and Vienna.

2000 *The Last Supper* premiered at the Staatsoper, Berlin, conducted by Barenboim. The production travels to Glyndebourne Touring Opera (conducted by Elgar Howarth) in the autumn and Glyndebourne Festival the following summer. Two full-length studies of his music published by Robert Adlington (*The Music of Harrison Birtwistle*, Cambridge University Press) and Jonathan Cross (*Harrison Birtwistle: Man, Mind, Music*, Faber & Faber).

2001 Boulez tours *Earth Dances* with Ensemble Modern Orchestra, opening three major festivals: musica viva in Munich, Wien Modern, and European Music Month in Basel. Made Companion of Honour by Queen Elizabeth II. Chairholder in Composition at University of Alabama (2001–2).

2002 Returns to the National Theatre to provide music for Sir Peter Hall's production of Euripides' *Bacchae*. *The Shadow of Night*, a Cleveland Orchestra commission, is premiered under Dohnányi in

Cleveland, with a subsequent performance at Carnegie Hall, New York. Teldec recording of *Pulse Shadows* wins Gramophone Award for Contemporary Music.

2003 *Theseus Game* for ensemble and two conductors premiered by Ensemble Modern at RUHRtriennale and by London Sinfonietta at Huddersfield Festival. *The Gleam*, a Christmas carol, premiered at the Christmas Eve Festival of Nine Lessons and Carols at King's College, Cambridge.

2004 Featured composer at Aldeburgh Festival, including premiere of chamber opera *The Io Passion*. Featured composer at Lucerne Festival, including *Night's Black Bird* commissioned as a companion piece to *The Shadow of Night*. An extended seventieth-birthday celebration under the title 'Birtwistle Games' is held at the Southbank Centre, including a major retrospective of his music and an exhibition of some of his 'falling line' drawings.

2006 Begins series of *Bogenstrich* ('bow-stroke') compositions for various combinations of cello, voice and piano.

2008 *The Minotaur* premiered by the Royal Opera, Covent Garden, conducted by Antonio Pappano. Production subsequently released on DVD by Opus Arte. His string quartet, *The Tree of Strings*, is premiered by Arditti Quartet in Witten and then toured around Europe.

2009 *The Corridor*, a new music-theatre piece based on the story of Orpheus and Eurydice, initiates the

Britten Studio at the Aldeburgh Festival, with further stagings at the London Southbank Centre, Holland Festival, Bregenz Festival and in the USA. Act 2 of *The Mask of Orpheus* given semi-staged performance at the BBC Proms to mark his seventy-fifth birthday. Full-length study of *The Mask of Orpheus* by Jonathan Cross published (Ashgate).

2010 The cantata *Angel Fighter* premiered at the Leipzig BachFest in the Thomaskirche. Made Honorary Doctor of Music by Cambridge University, to add to similar honours already received from City, Hull, London, Manchester, Salford and Sussex Universities.

2011 Christian Tetzlaff premieres Violin Concerto with the Boston Symphony Orchestra, followed by the European premiere at the BBC Proms. *In Broken Images* (after Gabrieli) premiered by London Sinfonietta in Milan and Turin to mark 150th anniversary of the unification of Italy. NMC recording of *Night's Black Bird* (disc also containing *The Shadow of Night* and *The Cry of Anubis*) wins Gramophone Award for Contemporary Music.

2012 Appointed Visiting Professor at the Royal Academy of Music. Complete string quartets recorded by Arditti Quartet on Aeon label. *Gigue Machine* for solo piano premiered by Nicolas Hodges in Stuttgart and played at the BBC Proms. Death of his wife Sheila. Full-length study of his theatre works published by David Beard (*Harrison Birtwistle's Operas and Music Theatre*, Cambridge University

Press). Premiere in Amsterdam of *The Moth Requiem*.

2013 Revival of *The Minotaur* at The Royal Opera in London (January). *Songs from the Same Earth*, song cycle for Mark Padmore, premiered at Aldeburgh Festival (13 June). *Construction with Guitar Player*, for solo guitar, completed.

2014 *Responses: sweet disorder and the carefully careless*, concerto for piano and orchestra, completed (January). Eightieth birthday (15 July).

With thanks to Jonathan Cross, Professor of Musicology at the University of Oxford, who prepared this timeline for Boosey & Hawkes and has given permission for it to be used here in a shortened form.

HARRISON BIRTWISTLE BIBLIOGRAPHY

R. Henderson, 'Harrison Birtwistle', *Musical Times*, CV (1964), 188–9

R. Smalley, 'Birtwistle's "Chorales"', *Tempo*, no. 80 (1967), 25–7

G. Crosse, 'Birtwistle's *Punch and Judy*', *Tempo*, no. 85 (1968), 24–6

R. Smalley, 'Birtwistle's *Nomos*', *Tempo*, no. 86 (1968), 7–10

M. Nyman, 'Two New Works by Birtwistle', *Tempo*, no. 88 (1969), 47–50

M. Chanan, 'Birtwistle's *Down by the Greenwood Side*', *Tempo*, no. 89 (1969), 19–21

M. Bowen, 'Harrison Birtwistle', *British Music Now: a Guide to the Work of Younger Composers*, ed. L. Foreman (London, 1975), 60–70

M. Hall, 'Birtwistle in Good Measure', *Contact*, no. 26 (1983), 34–6

A. Clements, 'Harrison Birtwistle: a Progress Report at 50', *Musical Times*, CXXV (1984), 136–9

M. Hall, *Harrison Birtwistle* (London, 1984)

P. Griffiths, 'Harrison Birtwistle', in *New Sounds, New Personalities: British Composers of the 1980s* (London, 1985), 86–94

E. Howarth, '*The Mask of Orpheus*', *Opera*, XXXVII (May 1986), 492–5

W. Mellers, *The Masks of Orpheus: Seven Stages in the Story of European Music* (Manchester, 1987)

T. Morgan, 'Birtwistle's *The Mask of Orpheus*', *New Music '87*, ed. M. Finnissy and R. Wright (Oxford, 1987), 76–8

M. Hall, 'The Sanctity of the Context: Birtwistle's Recent Music', *Musical Times*, CXXIX (1988), 14–16

J. Cross, 'Issues of Analysis in Birtwistle's Four Songs of Autumn', in *New Music '89*, ed. M. Finnissy and R. Wright (Oxford, 1989), 16–23

R. Samuel, 'Gawain's Musical Journey', Royal Opera House programme book (May 1991); rev. as '*Gawain*: an Essay and a Diary', *Cambridge Opera Journal*, IV (1992), 163–78

A. Ford, 'The Reticence of Intuition – Sir Harrison Birtwistle', in *Composer to Composer: Conversations about Contemporary Music* (London, 1993), 52–9

A. Whittall, 'The Geometry of Comedy', *Musical Times*, CXXXIV (1993), 17–19

J. Cross, 'The Challenge of Modern Music: Birtwistle's *Refrains and Choruses*', in *Theory, Analysis and Meaning in Music*, ed. A. Pople (Cambridge, 1994), 184–94

J. Cross, 'Lines and Circles: on Birtwistle's *Punch and Judy* and *Secret Theatre*', *Music Analysis*, XIII (1994), 203–25

J. Cross, 'The Action Never Stops, it Only Changes [*The Second Mrs Kong*]', *Musical Times*, CXXXV (1994), 698–703

R. Samuel, 'Time Remembered: Birtwistle's *The Second Mrs Kong*', *Opera*, XLV (1994), 1153–8

A. Whittall, 'Comparatively Complex: Birtwistle, Maxwell Davies and Modernist Analysis', *Music Analysis*, XIII (1994), 139–59

D. Wright, 'Clicks, Clocks and Claques: the Achievement of Harrison Birtwistle at 60', *Musical Times*, CXXXV (1994), 426–31

R. Adlington, 'Harrison Birtwistle's Recent Music', *Tempo*, no. 196 (1996), 2–8

D. Bruce, 'Challenging the System [*Panic*]', *Musical Times*, CXXXVII (1996), 11–16

J. Cross, 'Birtwistle's Secret Theatres', in *Analytical Strategies and Musical Interpretation: Essays on Nineteenth- and Twentieth-Century Music*, ed. C. Ayrey and M. Everist (Cambridge, 1996), 207–25

S. Pettitt, 'Birtwistle's Secret Theatres', *Opera*, XLVII (1996), 366–9

C. Wintle: 'A Fine & Private Place', *Musical Times*, no. 1845 (1996), 5–8

H. Birtwistle, in conversation with R. Lorraine, 'Territorial Rites 1', *Musical Times*, CXXXVIII (1997), 4–8; 'Territorial Rites 2', *Musical Times*, CXXXVIII/ Nov (1997), 12–16

A. Whittall, 'Modernist Aesthetics, Modernist Music: Some Analytical Perspectives', *Music Theory in Concept and Practice*, ed. J. M. Baker, D. W. Beach and J. W. Bernard (Rochester NY, 1997), 157–80

M. Hall, *Harrison Birtwistle in Recent Years* (London, 1998)

A. Whittall, 'Orpheus – and After', *Musical Times*, no. 1865 (1998), 55–8

A. Whittall, 'The Mechanisms of Lament: Harrison Birtwistle's *Pulse Shadows*', *Music and Letters*, LXXX (1999), 86–102

R. Adlington, *The Music of Harrison Birtwistle* (Cambridge, 2000)

D. Beard, 'An Analysis and Sketch Study of the Early Instrumental Music of Sir Harrison Birtwistle (*c.* 1957–77)' (D.Phil. disseration, University of Oxford, 2000)

J. Cross, *Harrison Birtwistle: Man, Mind, Music* (London, 2000)

D. Beard, 'From the Mechanical to the Magical: a Pre-Compositional Plan for Birtwistle's *Carmen arcadiae mechanicae perpetuum*', Mitteilungen der Paul Sacher Stiftung, XIV (2001), 29–33

M. Taylor, 'Narrative and Musical Structures in Harrison Birtwistle's *The Mask of Orpheus* and *Yan Tan Tethera*', in *Musiktheater heute*, ed. H. Danuser and M. Kassel (Mainz, 2003), 173–93

D. Beard, 'The Endless Parade: Competing Narratives in Recent Birtwistle Studies', *Music Analysis*, XXIII (2004), 89–127

D. Beard, 'The Shadow of Opera: Dramatic Narrative and Musical Discourse in *Gawain*', *twentieth-century music*, 2 (2005), 159–95

D. Beard, '"A Face like Music": Shaping Images into Sound in *The Second Mrs Kong*', *Cambridge Opera Journal*, XVIII (2006), 273–300

D. Beard, 'Beauty and the Beast: a Conversation with Sir Harrison Birtwistle', *Musical Times*, no. 1902 (2008), 9–25

D. Beard, 'Birtwistle's Labyrinth [*The Minotaur*]', *Opera*,
   LIX (2008), 372–81

J.-P. Heberlé, 'Réécritures du mythe d'Orphée et enjeux
   esthétiques, philosophiques et formels dans *The Mask of
   Orpheus* de Harrison Birtwistle', Revue LISA, VI (2008),
   http://lisa.revues.org/index1126.html

J. Cross, *Harrison Birtwistle's The Mask of Orpheus*
   (Farnham, 2009)

D. Beard, *Harrison Birtwistle's Operas and Music Theatre*
   (Cambridge, 2012)

ACKNOWLEDGEMENTS

Many people have given support, some in ways they may not have realised: David Allenby, Tony Bell, Ralph Blackbourn, Felicity Bryan, Silvia Crompton, Jonathan Cross, David Harsent, Alina Ibragimova, Jennifer Johnston, Oliver Knussen, Colin Matthews, Caroline Mustill, Tom Mustill, Andrew Rosner, Tom Service, Janis Susskind, John Tomlinson, Mitsuko Uchida, Patrick Wright. Michael Downes as copy-editor was patient and vigilant; so too was Jill Burrows, as typesetter, indexer and proofreader. Carol McDaid cast her hawk-eye over the manuscript at a late stage. With ever loving thanks to Tom Phillips, for reading and remembering. Belinda Matthews at Faber & Faber was unstinting in her enthusiasm and support at every stage – a writer's dream editor.

Chief thanks goes to all Birtwistles: Adam, Silas and Toby talked freely about their father and, helped by Harry's grandson Cecil, dug out family photographs now being shown in public for the first time. At all times they were warm, helpful and funny. Thank you above all to Harry. He allowed his space, time and quietude to be invaded, and trusted me to get on with it.

INDEX

Accrington and district, 5–11,
13–14, 17, 19, 36, 38, 49–51,
62, 79–80, 138–9, 206, 221,
252, 268–71, 285
Accrington Clef Club, 9
Accrington Observer, 3
Adès, Thomas, 182
Adlington, Robert: *The Music of
Harrison Birtwistle*, 292
Aeschylus: *The Oresteia*, 16, 83–5,
289
Afghanistan, 3
Agar, Ashton, 179
Aimard, Pierre-Laurent, xii
Alabama, University of, 292
Aldeburgh Festival, 60, 68, 70, 96,
149, 150, 154, 198, 286, 287,
293, 294
Britten Studio, 294
Red House, 149
Snape Maltings Concert Hall,
70, 149
Alexander the Great, 16
Alexander Nevsky (film), 37
Amadeus Quartet, 224
Anderson, Barry, 289
Anne, Princess Royal, 91
Anstey Combe, Wiltshire
(Birtwistle home), 189
Architectural Association, 251
Arditti Quartet, 293, 294
Asbury, Stefan, 125, 128
Atherton, David, 128, 205, 211
Athos, Mount, 231

Auden, W. H., 39–40, 91, 138
Ax, Emanuel, 190

Bach, Johann Sebastian, 64,
116–17, 133, 134, 136, 137,
275, 280
The Art of Fugue, 64, 275
cantatas, 116
chorale preludes, 137
Concerto in D minor for two
violins (BWV1043), 117
Little Organ Book, 136
The Musical Offering, 64, 275
Wachet auf (BWV140), 117
The Well-tempered Clavier, 275
Bacon, Francis, 23, 94
Bambi (film), 37
Baptist Hymnal, 279
Barbican Centre, London, 153, 290
Barbirolli, John, 26, 70, 266
Barenboim, Daniel, 128, 197,
206, 292
Bayreuth Festival, 206
BBC, 50, 97, 140, 288, 290
Third Programme, 51
BBC Promenade Concerts, 131,
218, 222, 239–40, 287, 291,
292, 294
BBC Singers, 218
BBC Symphony Orchestra, 242,
287, 288, 290
Beano, 50
Beard, David: *Harrison Birtwistle's
Operas and Music Theatre*, 294